GABRIEL

About the Author

Richard Webster (New Zealand) travels around the world lecturing and conducting workshops on psychic subjects. He is the author of more than two dozen books, including *Palm Reading for Beginners, Feng Shui for Beginners, Spirit Guides & Angel Guardians, The Encyclopedia of Superstitions,* and *Candle Magic for Beginners.*

COMMUNICATING WITH THE
ARCHANGEL

GABRIEL

FOR INSPIRATION & RECONCILIATION

Richard Webster

Llewellyn Publications
Woodbury, Minnesota

First Edition
Fifth Printing, 2011

Book design by Michael Maupin
Cover illustration ©2004, Neal Armstrong / Koralik & Associates
Cover design by Gavin Dayton Duffy
Edited by Connie Hill

Library of Congress Cataloging-in-Publication Data
Webster, Richard, 1946 –
    Gabriel : communicating with the archangel for inspiration & reconciliation / Richard Webster. — 1st ed.
        p.   cm.
    Includes bibliographical references and index.
    ISBN 13: 978-0-7387-0641-2
    ISBN 10: 0-7387-0641-8
    1. Gabriel (Archangel)—Miscellanea. 2. Spiritual life—Miscellanea.
    I. Title.
BF1999.W419   2004
202'.15—dc22   2004063748

Llewellyn Publications
A Division of Llewellyn Worldwide Ltd.
2143 Wooddale Drive
Woodbury, MN 55125-2989
www.llewellyn.com
Llewellyn is a registered trademark of Llewellyn Worldwide Ltd.
Printed in the United States of America

The Archangels Series
by Richard Webster

Gabriel
Michael
Raphael
Uriel

Also available in Spanish

Other Books by Richard Webster

For my good friends,
Dusty and Mary Cravens

CONTENTS

Introduction

ANGELS are beings composed of spirit. Their main purpose is to serve and worship God. They also carry out missions from God, and serve humanity in a wide variety of ways, such as revealing divine truths and helping people gain salvation.

Angels are able to change shape, and have appeared to humans in the guise of men, women, and children. In fact, the popular picture of an angel is of a being who is beautiful, young, and wearing flowing robes, a halo, and large wings. This might be an accurate description some of the time, but angels have the ability to appear in any form they wish.

Angels are genderless, but contain the finest qualities of both men and women to enable them to serve God in the best possible way. They are immortal, in the sense that they do not die as we do. However, they are not eternal, as only God is eternal.

The word "angel" is derived from the Greek word *angelos*, which means "messenger." In 1951 Pope Pius XII declared Archangel Gabriel the patron saint of postal workers, which means the supreme messenger looks after the people who deliver messages. Gabriel is the perfect choice for this, as in an old Jewish legend she introduced herself to Abraham by saying, "I am the angel Gabriel, the messenger of God."[1] Also, of course, Gabriel brought the most important message of all when she visited the Virgin Mary and told her that she would give birth to Jesus Christ.[2]

Angels have been working as divine messengers for thousands of years. They are considered to be intermediaries between God and mankind in the religious traditions of most faiths, and are still fulfilling that role today. Of course, they also mediated between Jesus and the heavenly Father.

However, angels are much more than beings who simply distribute messages. They constantly attend the throne of God (Genesis 32:1; Psalms 103:21; 1 Kings 22:19; Job 1:6). They possess a strong sense of right and wrong (2 Samuel 14:17). They rejoice every time a sinner repents. However, they will, when necessary, punish the wicked (Genesis 22:11; Exodus 14:19; Numbers 20:16; Psalms 34:7). They also protect the good. They keep company with people when they pray, and carry the souls of the just to heaven. They can change their form when, and if, required. The enduring words: "Be not forgetful to entertain strangers: for thereby some have entertained angels unawares"

(Hebrews 13:2) relate to this. The angels work ceaselessly for God, and will be present at His second coming.

In the Islamic tradition, two angels are assigned to everyone at birth. One records the person's good deeds, while the other writes down the bad ones. Fortunately, the evil deeds are not recorded until after the person has fallen asleep, as this allows him or her some hours in which to repent. If this occurs, the record shows that God has pardoned him or her.

Angels are, of course, also responsible for looking after the good and the innocent. The early Christian fathers taught that every human being is appointed a guardian angel at birth. The angel performs this task, not only as a duty to God, but also from feelings of love for the person he or she is protecting. The guardian angel works for his or her human until the person's soul is carried to heaven. If necessary the guardian angel will visit his charge in purgatory. In *The Divine Comedy*, Dante describes how souls in purgatory were comforted by their guardian angels.[3] Raphael is considered the prince of guardian angels.

Jesus expressed a belief in angels (Matthew 26:53; John 1:51), and was helped by them in moments of crisis. In Matthew 4:11 angels came and ministered to him after he had been tempted by the devil. At the Mount of Olives, Jesus knelt down and prayed, "Saying, 'Father, if thou be willing, remove this cup from me: nevertheless not my will, but thine, be done.' And there appeared an angel unto him from heaven, strengthening him" (Luke 22: 42–43).

The early Christian church was extremely interested in anything to do with angels, and scholars immediately tried to classify them into groups, or hierarchies. The best known of these was created in the sixth century by Dionysius, the Areopagite, in a book called *The Celestial Hierarchies*. Most of the later arrangements of angels were based on his work. His sequence is:

1. Seraphim

2. Cherubim

3. Thrones

4. Dominions

5. Virtues

6. Powers

7. Principalities

8. Archangels

9. Angels

In many ways, this list is surprising, as archangels are in the second to last position. They are also placed in this position in the hierarchies created by St. Ambrose, St. Jerome, St. Gregory, and John of Damascus. However, there are archangels on each side of God's throne, showing their importance. Dionysius arranged his angels deliberately. The higher ones carried out cosmic concerns, while the lower ones looked after matters on the earth.

The Christian Church found angels a difficult subject to deal with. The first Ecumenical Council in 325 CE accepted angels as a reality, and decreed that people should make use of the angelic world to reach heaven. However, less than twenty years later this was rescinded, as the council members thought that any interest in angels took the emphasis away from Christ. In 787 CE the Seventh Ecumenical Synod came to the conclusion that angels can act as liaisons between God and mankind.

In the thirteenth century St. Thomas Aquinas (1225–1274) wrote his *Summa Theologica*, which explained angel communication, how they traveled, and why they were essential to life on earth. He believed that angels were pure intellect, but could use mental energy to create a physical form whenever necessary.

In the eighteenth century Emanuel Swedenborg (1688–1772), an eminent Swedish scientist and philosopher, wrote a number of books about his communications with angels and his visits to heaven. He felt that only a few people have the opportunity to speak with angels directly, but that everyone can benefit by learning more about them.

Interest in angels gradually declined after the time of Swedenborg, and even in the Christian churches they become something of an embarrassment. However, in the last few decades interest has increased dramatically and polls show that 69 percent of Americans believe in angels, and 46 percent feel they have a guardian angel who looks after them. Thirty-two percent of Americans have felt an angelic presence.[4] I am sure these percentages will increase as more and more people become introduced to the world of angels. Certainly, there appear to be more and more angelic encounters, even among people who have not previously shown any interest in the subject.

Archangels are individualized spirits who are more involved with the overall picture than with the details. They are concerned about mankind as a whole, rather than in individual members of the human race. This is why archangels often look after entire nations, as they are concerned about the survival and well-being of the country, rather than the millions of individual people who happen to live there.

The main characteristics of the four best-known archangels are well known. Michael is in charge of the celestial army, and is frequently seen in works of art fighting a serpent or dragon, which symbolizes Satan. He brings courage and leadership. Gabriel is God's messenger, and is usually depicted in this role in works of art. The Annunciation, in which Gabriel told Mary that she was to give birth to a son, is the prime example of this. Gabriel provides inspiration, intuition, and communication. Raphael is the guardian of humanity, and is often depicted as a pilgrim or traveller. He is the divine physician, and brings compassion and healing. Uriel is the interpreter of prophecies, and usually carries a scroll or book. Uriel is usually shown meeting the disciples on the road to Emmaus (Luke 24:13–35). Uriel provides divine peace and devotion.

Each archangel has a specific area of responsibility, and is usually concerned with the larger picture. Their task is to help humanity as a whole. However, they are also willing to help you whenever you need it. If you need help or guidance, all you need to do is ask.

The purpose of this book is to show you how to work with Gabriel. She is willing to help you overcome your limitations and achieve your goals. There is also a slight possibility that she may ask you to help her in some way. If this happens, it will be because she has chosen you to perform a task that will benefit everyone.

Once you welcome angels and archangels into your life, you will always be aware of angelic visitations, and your life will be enhanced and enriched in many different ways.

Gabriel is waiting. In chapter one we'll look at her history and what she represents. After we have covered that, we will move on to discuss the various ways in which you can communicate with Gabriel. None of this will make your life perfect, but regular communication with Gabriel will ensure that you stay on track and fulfill your purpose in this incarnation.

One

WHO IS GABRIEL?

And in the sixth month the angel Gabriel was sent from God unto a city of Galilee, named Nazareth, to a virgin espoused to a man whose name was Joseph, of the house of David; and the virgin's name *was* Mary. And the angel came in unto her, and said, "Hail, *thou that art* highly favoured, the Lord is with thee: blessed *art* thou among women." And when she saw *him*, she was troubled at his saying, and cast in her mind what manner of salutation this should be. And the angel said unto her, "Fear not, Mary: for thou hast found favour with God. And, behold, thou shalt conceive in thy womb, and bring forth a son, and shalt call his name JESUS."

—Luke 1:26–31

GABRIEL is one of only two angels mentioned by name in the Bible. (The other is Michael. Raphael is mentioned in the *Apocrypha*, which is included in the Catholic Bible.) Gabriel, Michael, and Raphael are the only three archangels recognized by the Roman Catholic Church. The name "Gabriel" means "God is my strength" or "God is mighty." The names of all the archangels finish with "el." *El* means brightness or shining. *Gabri* means "governor." Consequently, a direct translation of Gabriel's name means "governor of light." In the *History of Joseph the Carpenter*, Gabriel is called "the herald of light."[1]

Gabriel In the Christian Tradition

Gabriel appears in the Bible as a messenger on important occasions. The most famous example of this is when she visited the Virgin Mary and told her to prepare for the birth of Jesus Christ (Luke 1:26–38). The famous Catholic prayer "Hail Mary" is believed to be the greeting that Gabriel used when visiting Mary.[2] The Koran (Surah 3: 45–51) also includes an account of this meeting, which is known as the Annunciation.

Gabriel also appeared to Zacharias to tell him that he and his wife Elizabeth should prepare for the birth of John the Baptist (Luke 1:5–25). An ancient legend says that Gabriel also announced the birth of Samson. Because of her close association with maternity, Gabriel is sometimes referred to as the Angel of Hope, and women seeking to become pregnant sometimes call on her for aid. In the Jewish tradition, it is also believed that Gabriel instructs the baby during the nine months it spends in the womb.

Many Christians also believe that Gabriel played a major role in at least three other important incidents concerning Jesus. They believe that it was Gabriel who announced Christ's birth to the shepherds. It was also Gabriel who warned Mary and Joseph that Herod's soldiers were searching for the newborn king. Finally, after the Resurrection, many people believe that it was Gabriel who rolled away the stone that was used to seal the tomb of Jesus.

Gabriel also made an earlier appearance in the Bible when she helped Daniel understand the symbolism of his strange dreams (Daniel 8:16–27). Daniel had dreamed of a ram with two horns, which was defeated by a he-goat with one horn. Gabriel told him that the ram symbolized the empire of the Medes and the Persians. The he-goat symbolized the king of the Greeks who would come and destroy them. Ultimately, this new kingdom would be divided into four parts. This vision came true almost two hundred years later when Alexander the Great and his army took over most of the known world. Gabriel visited Daniel again to tell him about the coming Messiah and the destruction of Jerusalem (Daniel 9: 21–27). Because of this, Gabriel is considered the archangel of dreams, premonitions, and clairvoyance.

A fascinating story about Gabriel concerns a letter that she allegedly wrote in 78 CE that contained "the commandments of Jesus Christ." This obviously forged letter became a relic of the early church, and an entire history of it was created. Apparently the letter, along with correspondence to and from Jesus, was found in 98 CE under a large rock, which a small child was able to move. Inscribed on the underside of this rock were the words "Blessed is he that shall turn me over."

Apparently these letters, written in Hebrew, were still in existence in the early nineteenth century. However, the originals have never been produced. Copies of the letters were sold in England as lucky charms, and were believed to provide safety in childbirth, and protect against "pestilence, lightning, thunder, and other evils, as certified by the words of Jesus himself."[3]

One old monastic text tells how the devil impersonated Gabriel:

"The devil appeared to a brother disguised as an angel of light and said to him, 'I am Gabriel and I have been sent to you.' The brother said to him, 'See if it is not someone else to whom you have been sent; as for me, I am not worthy of it'—and immediately the devil vanished."[4]

In medieval times, the *Angelus*, or Ave, bell was frequently known as the Gabriel Bell. The Angelus is a Roman Catholic devotion that is recited three times a day, usually at 6 AM, noon and 6 PM. The Angelus bell is rung at these times, honoring the Annunciation. The prayer starts with the words: *Angelus Domini nuntiavit Mariae*, which means: "The angel of the Lord brought tidings to Mary."

Much later, it is believed that Gabriel visited Joan of Arc and encouraged her to help the Dauphin, and start progressing in a career that included rescuing Orléans from the British in 1431.

According to a nineteenth-century sect called the Harmonists, Gabriel appeared to their leader, Father George Rapp (1757–1847), in New Harmony, Indiana, and even left her footprint on a limestone slab that can still be seen in the yard of the Maclure-Owen residence.[5]

In 1862, in New Zealand, Gabriel visited the Maori prophet Te Ua Haumene and gave him the strength to free himself from the ropes that imprisoned him. Te Ua later said that Gabriel, Michael, and "an innumerable host of ministering spirits" had appeared around him.[6]

In the Christian tradition, it is Gabriel who blows the horn to wake the dead on Judgment Day. Muslims believe this task will be performed by Israfel. Cole Porter used this theme for the song *Blow, Gabriel, Blow* in his 1934 musical *Anything Goes.*

Gabriel In the Islamic Tradition

In Islamic tradition, Gabriel is believed to have taught Noah how to build his ark. Gabriel also ordered the angels of safety to bring Noah timber from the famed cedar trees of Lebanon. Noah built his boat using one hundred and twenty-four thousand planks, and on each one was inscribed the name of one of the prophets. God sent an angel to inspect each individual plank in the ark to ensure that it was sound.

Gabriel, as Gibrail, or Djibril, which is the Islamic masculine equivalent of Gabriel, also appeared to the prophet Muhammad and dictated the Koran to him, chapter by chapter. Sometimes, Gabriel appeared to Muhammad in the shape of different people, but on one memorable occasion Muhammad asked if he could see her as she actually was. At the appointed time, Gabriel stood with her wings outstretched, and her shape filled the entire sky. Once he saw Gabriel in a cloud, and on another occasion she demonstrated her power by beating six hundred wings.[7]

In the Islamic tradition, Michael is considered to be five hundred years older Gabriel. He is also considered to be Gabriel's senior. In heaven, it is Gabriel who calls people to prayer, but Michael who conducts the prayers.

Before he received the call from Allah, Muhammad used to spend much of his time meditating in a mountain cave called Hira, a few miles northeast of Mecca. He was in this cave when Archangel Gabriel appeared to him with the news that God had chosen him to lead mankind back into the path of righteousness. Apparently, after Gabriel's first visit, Muhammad returned to his wife Khadija, concerned about the experience. However, after Gabriel's second visit, Muhammad returned home, aware of what he had to do. The religion of Islam was the result. Khadija was Muhammad's first convert to Islam.

The Moslems also believe that it was Gabriel who presented Abraham with the Black Stone of the Kaba. Moslems who make the annual pilgrimage to Mecca kiss this stone. Incidentally, it is believed that this stone was originally white, but gradually turned black as it absorbed all the sins of humanity. In the Hadîth, one of the most important sacred books of Islam, Gabriel is referred to as *al-Námūs al-akbar*, which means "the great angel who is entrusted with secret messages."

When Muhammad ascended to heaven, Gabriel, the Islamic angel of truth, guided him through all seven heavens. At each of the heavens he was greeted by a Biblical prophet. Moses greeted him at the entrance to the sixth heaven, and when Muhammad passed on, Moses wept. Someone asked him why, and Moses replied: "I weep because of a youth (Muhammad) who has been sent after me, more of whose community will enter Paradise than my community."[8]

A fascinating Sufi story tells how Gabriel helped Moses write the Torah on tablets of gold. God sent Gabriel and ninety-nine other angels to help him reach the required state of purity to do this. Each angel represented an aspect of God, and they taught him 124,000 words. With each new word, Moses was raised to a new level until he could see only pure light. Once he had reached this desired state, Gabriel told the other angels to fill Moses with the specific attributes they carried. Then Gabriel filled Moses' heart with the knowledge that had to be written on the tablets. She also taught Moses how to make gold, and on the tablets he created, Moses wrote the Torah.[9]

Gabriel knows all the languages of the world, and in the course of a single night taught Joseph all seventy languages that were spoken in the Tower of Babel. This feat promoted Joseph, a humble slave, to the second most important person in the land, ahead of all the princes of Pharaoh.[10]

Like all angels, Gabriel can change appearance whenever necessary. When Abraham saw her, she was in the guise of a man, for instance. When she visited Muhammad, her body obscured half the sky. The experience of the Sufi Ruzbehan Baqli was totally different:

"In the first rank I saw Gabriel, like a maiden, or like the moon amongst the stars. His hair was like a woman's, falling in long tresses. He wore a red robe embroidered in green . . . He is the most beautiful of Angels . . . His face is like a red rose."[11]

One of the most astonishing stories about Gabriel is a Muslim tradition that she invented coffee. Apparently, Muhammad was extremely tired and ready to go to sleep. Gabriel brought him a cup of coffee, and this gave Muhammad the necessary strength to not only defeat forty horsemen, but also to satisfy forty women.

Gabriel In the Judaic Tradition

In the Talmud, the most important book of civil and religious law in the Jewish faith, Gabriel is shown as the destroyer of the hosts of Sennacherib. He is also one of the angels who buried Moses and showed Joseph the way.

Angels also play an important role in the Jewish Kabbalah. The midnight vigil is mentioned many times in the Zohar, and is considered a Kabbalistic exercise. Every night God enters Paradise to celebrate with the righteous. The trees start singing hymns, and a wind from the north carries a spark that strikes Archangel Gabriel beneath her wings. This spark is the divine fire of God. Gabriel cries out and wakes all the cocks, who start crowing. This wakes up the pious, who then study the Torah until dawn. The Kabbalists believe that spirits and demons possess power only until the cock crows.[12]

Gabriel is associated with the moon. According to an ancient Jewish legend, God, accompanied by Gabriel and Michael, taught Moses the intricacies of the calendar, including the different forms of the moon.[13] Each of the seven planets that could be seen by the ancients was given its own angel:

Sun—Raphael

Venus—Aniel

Mercury—Michael

Moon—Gabriel

Saturn—Kafziel

Jupiter—Zadkiel (Dionysius says he is an² arch.)
Fire

Mars—Sammael

Gabriel is associated with the element of water. (However, some traditions associate Gabriel with the element of Air, and in the *Third Book of Enoch* Gabriel is said to rule the Fire element.) This makes her archangel over streams, rivers, seas, and oceans. She watches over everyone who travels by sea. Because Water and the moon both symbolize the emotions, Gabriel also happens to be the archangel of emotions. The moon also represents femininity, and Gabriel looks after women as well as the feminine aspects of men. This association with the moon also means that Gabriel rules Monday, and has the moonstone as her gemstone.

According to Enoch, the archangels Michael and Gabriel live in the seventh heaven and stand on the right- and left-hand sides of God. However, Gabriel rules Makon, the sixth heaven, while Michael rules Arabot, the seventh heaven. In The Book of Enoch, Gabriel is described as one of the holy angels. She is in charge of Paradise, and of the Seraphim and Cherubim (Enoch 20:7). There has been a great deal of confusion about the use of the word "seraphim" in this verse, and it has been translated variously as "serpent" and "dragons."[14]

According to an old Babylonian legend, Gabriel was demoted for twenty-one days from her position in charge of the sixth heaven, and replaced by Dubbiel, the guardian angel of the Persians. Apparently Jehovah became angry with the Jewish people for some reason, and asked Gabriel to destroy the Jewish people. She was told to pour burning coals on top of them, and then allow the Babylonians to kill the survivors.

Gabriel felt sorry for the Israelites, probably because her colleague, Archangel Michael, was the guardian of the Israeli people. Because of this, she asked the laziest angel in heaven to help her. This angel took so long to pass the coals to Gabriel that they had cooled down by the time Gabriel threw them down to earth. Gabriel followed this by persuading the Babylonians not to kill the Jews. She suggested that they force the Jews into Babylon.

Not surprisingly, Jehovah was disappointed with Gabriel, and replaced her with Dubbiel. In the space of just a few weeks, with the help of Dubbiel, the Persians cruelly oppressed the Jewish people. This would have continued indefinitely, but fortunately, Gabriel gave God a good suggestion and was promoted back to her former position again. Dubbiel ultimately became one of the fallen angels.[15]

Although Enoch placed Michael and Gabriel on the right- and left-hand sides of God, the more usual arrangement is for the celestial throne to be surrounded by the four archangels, with Michael on the right, Uriel on the left, Raphael behind, and Gabriel in front. This dates back to the time of Moses.[16] However, the archangels have traditionally been related to the four cardinal directions and the four elements, and this creates a slightly different arrangement:

East	Air	Raphael
South	Fire	Michael
West	Water	Gabriel
North	Earth	Uriel

Two thousand years ago, Gabriel was considered the angel of war, and was sometimes referred to as the "severe angel." This was not surprising, as ancient Jewish legends tell how Gabriel destroyed Sennacherib's camp, demolished Sodom and Gomorrah, and set fire to the temple in Jerusalem.[17] She also wrestled Jacob for an entire night—although, to be fair, several other angels were also involved (Genesis 32: 24–32, Hosea 12:4). In fact, at one time Gabriel even came close to destroying the entire population of Israel. Fortunately, God reminded her that there were some good people living there.

Over time, this view of Gabriel gradually changed. In the Jewish tradition, Gabriel is believed to be in charge of the celestial treasury. John Milton expanded on this and made her the guardian of Heaven: "Betwixt these rocky pillars Gabriel sat, Chief of the angelic guards, awaiting night" (*Paradise Lost* IV:550).

In the Zohar II, 11a–11b, Gabriel is said to be in charge of the soul. When someone dies, it is Gabriel who receives the person's soul and takes it to its new home, which is determined by the past actions of the deceased. When it is time for the soul to reincarnate, Gabriel will accompany the spirit back to earth.

Gabriel in Art

Gabriel is a popular figure in religious works of art, and is usually shown carrying a lily or a trumpet. The lily comes from a verse in the *Song of Solomon* that is thought to signify Mary's purity: "I am the rose of Sharon, and the lily of the valleys" (Solomon 2:1). The trumpet is an obvious symbol of Judgment Day. Gabriel is shown blowing a trumpet in Judgment, the twentieth card of the Major Arcana of the Tarot deck.

Early paintings sometimes portray Gabriel with a scepter. Occasionally, she is depicted with a shield and a spear. Over the years, many artists, such as Leonardo da Vinci, Barbieri, Martini, Angelico, Raphael, Dante Gabriel Rossetti, and Peter Paul Rubens, who painted six versions of the Annunciation.

Surprisingly, until the eleventh century, artists seldom used the Annunciation as a subject. By the thirteenth century, it was one of the most common themes in religious art. In Italy, artists frequently painted Gabriel and the Virgin Mary on separate canvases. The two paintings were placed on opposite sides of the altar, with the Virgin Mary on the right-hand side and Gabriel on the left. Even when they shared the same painting, a pillar or other ornament usually kept them apart. In early paintings of the Annunciation, Gabriel is given the principal role. However, at about the beginning of the fourteenth century, the roles reversed and Mary became the main figure, with Gabriel taking a subservient role. Sometimes, Mary was shown sitting on a beautiful throne, wearing a crown of gems and flowers, as she accepted the message from Gabriel. There is a magnificent painting in the Louvre by Fra Bartolommeo (1472–1517) called "The Annunciation, with Saints Margaret, Mary Magdelen, Paul, John the Baptist, Jerome and Francis" (1515) that shows the Virgin Mary sitting on a throne.

Gabriel, holding a lily, is above her, descending to the ground. The saints give all their attention to the Virgin Mary. This painting clearly shows how popular and venerated Mary had become.

One sculpture of Gabriel that I particularly love is in the Cathedral of Reims in France. It is part of a huge grouping of sculptures that decorate a doorway. Each slightly elongated figure stands on its own pedestal, and looks perfectly at home in this enormous cathedral. Two of these sculptures depict the Annunciation. Gabriel is smiling at Mary, who looks solemn and concerned. Unfortunately, one of Gabriel's wings has been lost over the last eight hundred years, but despite the wear and tear of time, the figures still look fresh and inspiring. The expressions on the faces, the details of the clothing, and even the feathers on the surviving wing reveal the skill that these long-forgotten artists possessed.

Gabriel in Literature

Gabriel makes only an occasional appearance in literature. In John Milton's epic poem, *Paradise Lost*, she is responsible for capturing Satan, who refuses to answer any questions and flies back to Hell.

Gabriel is mentioned occasionally in the diaries of Dr. John Dee, the great Elizabethan philosopher and magician. On one occasion, Gabriel appeared and told John Dee that his wife Jane was pregnant, which was correct. She then gave Dee some advice on the difficulties Jane was having with the pregnancy. On July 13, 1584, Dee's fifty-seventh birthday, Gabriel appeared and told Dee that he possessed the keys to God's "storehouses . . . wherein you shall find (if you enter wisely, humbly and patiently) Treasures more worth than the frames of the heavens."[18]

In the first scene of *The Green Pastures,* a play by Marc Connelly that was first performed in 1930, Gabriel is shown helping God conduct his work in his celestial office in heaven. Gabriel picks up his trumpet and God warns him not to blow it until the Day of Judgment. Gabriel tells God that he hasn't visited earth in at least four hundred years. The rest of the play retells much of the story of Genesis, and finishes with God back in heaven surrounded by angels. He tells Gabriel that mercy comes through suffering, and even God must suffer.

Gabriel Today

Christopher Knight and Robert Lomas, authors of *The Second Messiah,* and *Uriel's Machine,* proposed an unorthodox, highly controversial scenario about Gabriel. Their theory is that angels were demoted from their original position of being gods themselves, and became mediators, acting as messengers between God and mankind. As such, they were sometimes described as being men. An example of this can be found in Joshua 5:13: "And it came to pass, when Joshua was by Jericho, that he lifted up his eyes and looked, and, behold, there stood a man over against him with his sword drawn in his hand." Because angels could become men, it was possible that when Gabriel visited the Virgin Mary to tell her she was to conceive, he inseminated her with his own godly seed.[19]

Today, Gabriel is considered to bring joy, love, happiness, and hope to the human race. She is also concerned with new starts, rejuvenation, resurrection, and rebirth. Because of her work with the Virgin Mary and Elizabeth, she is also believed to be involved with pregnancy and childbirth, doing whatever is necessary to help the mother. When a woman wants to conceive, Gabriel is prepared to help. The ancient Jews believed that Gabriel also instructed the baby while it was in the mother's womb. For all of these reasons, Gabriel is known as the Angel of Annunciation.

One of the most charming stories about Gabriel relates to her role as archangel of childbirth. Gabriel carefully chooses the souls in heaven who are due to be born. She teaches the unborn baby its mission in the physical incarnation, and then swears the baby to keep this knowledge secret. This silence is reinforced, because Gabriel presses her finger on the baby's lips, creating the cleft under the nose.

I also like the story about Gabriel that William Blake recorded in his diary. He had been commissioned to draw an angel, but was having difficulty. He asked himself, "Who can paint an angel?" Immediately, he heard a voice saying, "Michelangelo could." William Blake looked around, but could see no one. "How do you know?" he asked. The strange voice replied: "I know, for I sat for him. I am the Archangel Gabriel." William Blake was taken aback by this reply, but was still suspicious. After all, this voice could be an evil spirit masquerading as Gabriel. He asked for further evidence. "Can an evil spirit do this?" the voice replied.

William Blake immediately became aware of a bright shape, with large wings. The shape radiated with pure light. The angel grew larger and larger, and the roof of Blake's study opened up as Gabriel rose up into heaven. William Blake's diary recorded that Gabriel then "moved the universe." He does not explain exactly how this happened, but wrote that he was convinced that he had seen Gabriel.[20]

Gabriel aids visions, and can also help you get glimpses of the future. This dates back to the time when she helped Daniel understand his visions.

However, Gabriel is still strong and opposed to evil in every form. Traditionally, her direction is west. West is considered to be where evil dwells, because this is where the sun sets at night, covering the earth with darkness, which can be construed as being negative.

You can call on Gabriel for help whenever you feel downhearted, need to overcome doubt and fear, or desire guidance, inspiration, intuition, or purification. If you feel trapped, locked in, or are simply in a rut, call on Gabriel to help you change and start moving ahead again. Gabriel can help you control negative habits, such as gossiping or lying to yourself. Gabriel is prepared to heal the inner child. All you need to do is ask. Naturally, you can also ask Gabriel to send healing and help to anyone you know who needs it.

Doubt and Fear

It is impossible to lead a full and rich life when you are constantly being held back by doubts and fears. It is sad that so many people are afflicted with these. Self-doubt holds many people back from achieving their goals, and fears, frequently imaginary, keep people imprisoned within a small comfort zone of their own making. Fortunately, Gabriel can help you release these shackles if they are holding you back from realizing your dreams.

When I first met Lorraine, she was in her mid-forties, and had been living alone since her marriage had broken up ten years earlier. She was desperately lonely, and came to one of my psychic development classes mainly to meet like-minded people. She worked in the accounts department of a large insurance company. At lunchtime every day, she sat with several others in the firm's cafeteria. One of these was a man whom she liked, and she was certain that he liked her, too. However, every time he made an effort to get to know her better, she pushed him away. Although she was lonely, she was scared of starting another relationship.

Once Lorraine got to know Gabriel and realized that she was protecting and guiding her, she was able to gradually lower her guard, and the friendship slowly developed.

"It was silly, really," she told me later. "We were two lonely people, but because I was so full of fear I couldn't let anyone into my life. I'm lucky that Bill was so patient."

If fears, doubts, and worries are holding you back in any area of your life, ask Gabriel to help you resolve them.

Guidance

Gabriel wants you to lead a happy, fulfilled life and will offer guidance and aid whenever you ask for it. If you feel lost, and have no idea where you are going in life, ask

Gabriel for help. If you are planning a major move, or have an important decision to make, ask Gabriel. If you have met someone new and are thinking of starting a new relationship, ask Gabriel for guidance.

Brenda, a woman I worked with many years ago, had spent most of her career as a receptionist. She was tired of this, but had no idea what else she could do. Her sister had been moderately successful selling real estate, and encouraged Brenda to take it up, too. Brenda immediately turned down the offer, as she had never sold anything before. However, the thought stayed at the back of her mind. She had always been interested in houses, and her friends told her she had a talent at home decorating. It took her a whole year to do anything about it. After an extremely bad day at work, she asked Gabriel for guidance. One month later, she began work in her new career.

"It was the most amazing experience," she told me. "Gabriel reaffirmed everything I felt—that I was stale, bored, unfulfilled, and unhappy. She knew that I was more than ready for a change. When I mentioned real estate, she told me that I was well suited for it, and should get started right away. I took her advice, and haven't looked back since. I should have asked her years ago. It might be sad to find your true calling after the age of fifty, but I know plenty of people who will never find it. I tell them to speak with Gabriel."

If you are still looking for your true calling in life, ask Gabriel.

Inspiration

If you wish, Gabriel will bring messages to you. If you want to know about the future, ask Gabriel to keep you informed. The gift of prophecy can be yours, if you ask Gabriel to help. Gabriel will also give you advice in the form of dreams and visions. She will help you grow in knowledge and wisdom. Your spiritual growth and development will progress faster than ever before. (Archangel Uriel can also help you develop intuitively. People frequently call on Uriel when they want to learn practical skills, such as reading Tarot cards, and call on Gabriel to help them develop clairvoyance and premonition in the form of dreams.)

I first met Martin about twenty years ago when he attended one of my classes. He had been introduced to the psychic world by a former girlfriend, and now that the relationship had ended, was not sure how to develop his natural talents further. He was a tense and nervous person who found it hard to relax. This, coupled with his desire for instant results, held him back and caused enormous frustration. One day, he felt like giving up completely. He called on Gabriel, wanting to know why she wouldn't help him. Gabriel immediately responded by saying that she had been waiting for Martin to ask.

This simple exchange was the turning point. Martin began communicating with Gabriel regularly, and started receiving glimpses of future events. He became more relaxed and outgoing. He started growing spiritually, and his clairvoyant and precognitive gifts developed rapidly. He credits all of this to his regular sessions with Gabriel.

"Gabriel showed me the way," he told me. He tapped his forehead. "She unblocked my third eye, and let me see, really see, for the first time in my life. I'd hate to think what my life would be like without Gabriel."

Purification

Purification can be necessary for a number of reasons. If someone is harboring impure or negative thoughts, purification will help him or her get back on track again. If someone has been badly hurt and will not forgive the other person, or let go of the incident, purification is required. Victims of sexual assault frequently feel unclean or dirty and need purification. The same thing also applies to victims of psychic attack. People who are codependent or full of negativity need purification, too. People who gossip or deceive themselves also need purification. Consequently, there can be very few people who do not need purification at some stage in their lives.

Nicholas is one of the kindest and gentlest people I have ever met. He is now in his early sixties, and looks years younger than he did ten years ago when he finally released himself from his guilty secret. When he was a small boy he was sexually molested by a priest at the school he attended. The abuse was systematic and lasted for some years. Nicholas never told anyone about it until he started reading newspaper reports of other people who had had similar experiences. Even then, it took some time for him to be able to let go of the incredible feelings of guilt he still held about the abuse. In his mind, it was his fault that it happened.

When a friend told him to ask Gabriel to help purify and heal him, Nicholas laughed, as he had lost his faith more than forty years earlier. However, his friend persisted, and gradually Nicholas realized that he had to do something, and possibly Gabriel could help. It took time, and a great deal of patience on the part of his friend, but gradually Nicholas came to know Gabriel and ask for help.

"I wish I'd known about Gabriel when I was a young man," he told me. "My life would have been so different. I've carried around this burden of shame and disgrace my whole life. I'm so happy that I'm actually living my life free of this huge millstone. I feel as if I've recaptured some of my lost youth."

Helping Others

Just recently, I spent the evening with some old friends and heard about the problems their son Graydon was experiencing. He had studied accounting at college, but then decided not to be an accountant. He then studied psychology for a year, but lost interest. He traveled for a couple of years in an attempt to find himself, and had now returned home, but was aimless and lost. Graydon still had no idea what he wanted to do with his life.

I offered to contact Gabriel on his behalf. My friends were doubtful about this, but were happy for me to speak to Gabriel. Two weeks later, I received a phone call from my friends saying that Graydon had made some new friends who were "into angels," and he was asking Gabriel for help in finding a sense of direction. My friends thought this was a coincidence. Happily, coincidence or not, Graydon gained valuable insights from his meetings with Gabriel, and is now self-employed as a personal fitness trainer. Until he spoke with Gabriel, the thought of using the skills he had learned as an athlete had never occurred to him. He is now on track, and feels completely fulfilled.

Now that you know something about Gabriel, and how she can help you, it is time to learn how to contact her. We will start on this in the next chapter.

Two

HOW TO CONTACT GABRIEL

GABRIEL is prepared to help you whenever you need her aid. Naturally, you should not contact her for frivolous reasons, but when the need is important, Gabriel will always be there for you. In an emergency, all you need to do is call out to her. Most of the time, though, the matter will not be urgent, and you can enjoy a more leisurely communication with her. Here are several methods that you can use to contact Gabriel. Experiment with them all, and see which method, or methods, you find most helpful.

Gabriel Center

You will find it helpful to have a designated place that you use whenever you contact Gabriel. Over a period of time, this place will develop an atmosphere, almost an aura, that you will sense as soon as you walk into it. You will feel instantly relaxed, purified, and ready to talk to Gabriel.

You might be fortunate enough to have an entire room that you can dedicate to Gabriel, although it is more likely that only part of a room will be used for this purpose. If possible, choose somewhere quiet, where you can work in peace, and without interruption.

A friend of mine in Tokyo lives in an apartment the size of many people's closets. She sits on the floor in front of a small table that serves as a temporary altar when she communicates with Gabriel. The rest of the time the table is used for preparing and eating food, and for storing things. Use whatever you have.

In the summer months I prefer to communicate with Gabriel outdoors. There is something special about performing a ritual outdoors, surrounded by nature. If you choose to do this, find a pleasant place where you will not be disturbed.

The important thing is to find somewhere where you feel safe and comfortable. This place can be your Gabriel center.

Relaxation Ritual

Preparation

You need to be physically, mentally, and spiritually prepared to talk with Gabriel. If possible, have a leisurely bath or shower, and put on fresh clothes. You might choose to wear a robe, or even work skyclad (unclothed), if you wish.

The purpose of this is to separate your communication with Gabriel from your everyday world.

I enjoy going for a walk before communicating with Gabriel. This takes me away from the house and gives me a chance to clarify in my mind the matters I want to discuss with Gabriel. Sometimes I discover that Gabriel is walking with me, and the walk becomes a discussion.

You may want to play some peaceful music, burn incense, or light candles. It makes no difference what you do, as long as it helps you relax and does not interfere with the purpose of the ritual. I seldom play music when communicating with angels, as I find it distracting. I want to focus on the communication, and don't want to find myself humming along with the music. However, everyone is different. You should play music if you think that it will help you.

Relaxation

The next stage in the procedure is to make yourself as comfortable as possible. Ensure that the room is warm enough. Cover yourself with a blanket, if you feel you might get cold. Sit down in a comfortable chair, and then relax your body and mind. You will find this a simple matter if you have practiced self-hypnosis or meditation. If you have not done this sort of thing before, here are the stages of the process:

1. Close your eyes and take three deep breaths, holding each breath for a few seconds, before exhaling slowly.

2. Focus your attention on the toes on your left foot, and tell them to relax. Wait until you can actually feel them relaxing before proceeding further.

3. Relax the muscles of your left foot, and then allow the relaxation to spread over your ankles, up your calf muscles, and into your knee. There is no need to hurry with this. Take all the time you need. When you feel ready, allow the relaxation to move into your thighs and into your left buttock.

4. Repeat this procedure with your right leg, again starting with the toes, and letting the relaxation gradually spread up your leg.

5. Allow the relaxation to spread into your stomach and chest, and up to your shoulders. Feel the tension leaving your shoulders as the pleasant relaxation takes over.

6. Allow the relaxation to spread down your left arm until it reaches the tips of your fingers. Repeat with your right arm.

7. Relax the muscles in your neck, and then allow the pleasant relaxation to drift into your face and up to the top of your head. Pay special attention to the muscles around your eyes. These are the finest muscles in your whole body, and you will find that as you relax these muscles, every other part of your body will relax still further.

8. You are now totally relaxed. Mentally scan your body to make sure that there are no areas of tension left. Focus on any areas that need further help, until they are totally relaxed also.

9. When you are sure that every part of your body is relaxed, take another three slow, deep breaths, and enjoy the feelings of relaxation throughout your body. You are now ready to meet Gabriel.

Invitation

You are now totally relaxed and ready to ask Gabriel to join you. Spend a few moments thinking about your need to contact Gabriel. You might need reassurance, support, comfort, guidance, insight, or purification. Think what your life will be like once you receive this aid. Become aware of the feelings of happiness and fulfillment you will experience once Gabriel has taken care of your problem.

When you feel ready, take a deep breath and exhale slowly. Start speaking to Gabriel. You can do this silently or out loud. Tell her of your need for help. Explain the difficulty, and the efforts you have made to resolve it. Ask her for protection, guidance, and help.

Speak for as long as necessary to fully explain the problem. Of course, Gabriel will instantly know what is going on. However, it is necessary for you to clearly explain the situation as it helps clarify it in your own mind.

Pause once you have done this. You may sense Gabriel's presence. This can be experienced in many different ways. You may feel a sense of warmth, as if you are being enfolded by her wings. You may simply experience a sense of knowing that she is there. If you sense her presence, thank her for coming to your aid.

If you experience nothing, ask her to come to you. Speak from the heart. You might say something along these lines: "Gabriel, thank you for looking after me in the past. I'm grateful for your unceasing efforts, not only with me, but with everyone. Right now I have a problem that is too hard for me to handle, and I need your help. Please come to my aid, Gabriel. Please help me."

Again, pause and see what response you receive. Keep repeating your request until you become aware that Gabriel is with you. Be patient if you have not communicated with Gabriel before. Once you start talking with her regularly, you will have no difficulty in making contact. However, you might need some patience the first few times you attempt this.

Communication

Once you know that Gabriel is with you, thank her for her time, interest, support, and love. Ask her for help in solving your problem. Listen carefully to what she has to say. It is unlikely that you will hear her voice. The most usual form of communication is for thoughts and insights to come into your conscious mind. Ask Gabriel to clarify anything you do not understand.

By the end of the conversation you should know exactly what to do. If the problem involves someone else, you should know how to approach him or her to resolve the situation. If the problem involves letting go of negativity and purifying yourself, you should know exactly what to do to make it happen.

Once you feel confident that you can make the next step, thank Gabriel for her help. Do not get up immediately after saying goodbye. Remain comfortably seated or lying down for a few minutes while thinking about Gabriel and her advice. When you feel ready, open your eyes, stretch, and get up.

Naturally, this ritual can be done in bed at night, and I know a number of people who do this. However, I drift off to sleep far too easily, and find it hard to stay awake long enough to make any form of angelic contact. Consequently, I always do this ritual in a comfortable chair, or lying on the floor, as I am more likely to stay awake this way.

Other Methods

The relaxation method that we have just covered is the best method to start with. It is extremely beneficial in its own right, as it enables every cell in your body to relax. It is also a highly effective way to contact Gabriel, and bring her into your life.

However, this method is time-consuming, and you may not always have enough time to sit down and perform the relaxation ritual. Here are some other methods that I have found useful. Experiment with them. You are likely to find that you enjoy some methods more than others. You will also find that you experience better results with the methods that you prefer.

Invoking the Archangels

This ritual invokes Michael, Gabriel, Raphael, and Uriel. It is used mainly to gain insight and protection for yourself, people you know, and for all of humanity.

I like to stand while doing this ritual, but you can sit down in a straight-backed chair, if you prefer. Face east. Close your eyes and take three or four deep breaths. Visualize yourself surrounded by a pure white light of protection.

When you feel ready, invoke Michael, the archangel of the south. He stands by your right-hand side. You do this by saying the following words out loud:

"I now invoke the mighty and powerful Archangel Michael to stand at my right-hand side. Please grant me the strength, courage, integrity, and protection I need to fulfill my purpose in this incarnation. Please use your sword to cut away any doubts and negativity. Surround me with your protection, so that I may always work on the side of good. Thank you."

Pause for thirty seconds. Become aware of Michael standing beside you, and be alert for any insights or words that he may offer. When you feel ready, invoke Uriel to stand at your left-hand side. Use the following, or similar, words:

"I now invoke the mighty and powerful Archangel Uriel to stand on my left-hand side. Please release all my tensions, worries, and insecurities. Grant me tranquility and peace of mind. Help me to serve others, and to give and receive generously. Thank you."

Pause again for thirty seconds, and see if Uriel has a message for you. You will sense Uriel standing to your left. Smilingly acknowledge his presence, and remain alert for any wisdom or advice that he might offer. When you feel ready, invoke Raphael to stand in front of you.

"I now invoke the mighty and powerful Archangel Raphael to stand in front of me. Please fill me with wholeness and good health. Help me heal the wounds from the past. Please heal and restore every aspect of my being. Thank you."

Pause silently, and see if Raphael has a message for you. You are likely to sense the wholeness and unity he brings to your being, even if you do not receive a specific message. When you feel ready, ask Gabriel to stand behind you.

"I now invoke the mighty and powerful Archangel Gabriel to stand behind me. Please bring me insights and guidance, so that I may always walk in the light. Remove all my doubts and fears, and purify my body, mind, and spirit. Thank you."

Again pause to see if Gabriel has a message for you. Once you have done this, experience the different energies of the four archangels around you. Although they provide you with completely different energies, each is an aspect of the Divine Consciousness. Naturally, as human beings, we tend to visualize the archangels as powerful beings, probably giant-like, but otherwise much like us, draped in gorgeous robes, surrounding and protecting us. It makes no difference how you perceive the archangels. The important thing to remember when performing this ritual is that you are experiencing the divine.

Enjoy the feelings of peace, security, and bliss. When you feel ready, ask the archangels for help, guidance, and protection for you, your family and friends, your community, country, and the entire world. You will experience the response in different ways. You may feel as if a flash of electricity has passed right through you. You may notice a distinct change in the temperature of the room. You may experience a sense of knowing that everything you have asked for will be granted.

Enjoy the comfort and security of the archangels' company for as long as you wish. When you feel ready to return to the everyday world, thank each of the archangels in turn, starting with Gabriel, and following with Uriel, Michael, and Raphael. You will sense each one leaving. When you feel ready, take a few deep breaths and count from one to five. Open your eyes and carry on with your day. You will feel invigorated and full of energy after this ritual.

I was able to handle a stressful time in my life much more easily by performing this ritual every day for several weeks. However, you do not need to wait until you need angelic help. Perform this ritual frequently, but do not waste the archangels' time with frivolous requests. Think carefully beforehand, and use your time with the archangels wisely.

Guidance Ritual

Gabriel is willing to provide guidance whenever you wish. Here is an effective ritual that enables you to receive the benefit of her advice whenever necessary.

Start by enjoying a pleasant walk. Ideally, this should be outdoors, but weather conditions might force you to remain indoors. Alternatively, you might like to drive to a shopping mall and walk under cover there.

While you are walking, look around and see how many things you can see that you are grateful for. You might be grateful for sunlight, the colors of fall, bookstores, automobiles, birds, grassy meadows, and the laughter of children. Obviously, if you are walking around your home you would come up with a different list. You might, for instance, give thanks for electric light, carpets, modern-day bathrooms, toothbrushes, and comfortable beds. Naturally, the things you are grateful for need not be "things." You might give thanks for a warm smile, a gentle hand on your shoulder, a cooling breeze, and the gurgling sound of a stream. See how many blessings you can come up with during the course of your walk.

Walk for at least fifteen minutes. Half an hour would be even better. When you return home, sit down in a comfortable chair, close your eyes, and run through your list of things to be grateful for. Visualize each one of them in your mind.

Once you have done this, it is time to think about your need for guidance. Think about the problem in general terms. You might be wondering whether or not to take a certain course at college. You might be thinking about buying a house, having another child, or starting a new relationship. Most of the time, the problem will be one that you have not been able to resolve yourself, which is why you are calling on Gabriel. Alternatively, you may have reached a decision, and now want Gabriel's approval of it before you proceed. It makes no difference what area of life you need guidance in. Gabriel will be happy to provide it.

Take three deep breaths, holding each breath for a few moments, before exhaling slowly. In your mind, ask Gabriel to join you. You might say something similar to this:

"Blessed Archangel Gabriel, thank you for all the blessings in my life. I am grateful for your guidance, inspiration, and purification. Please come to me, as I need your help."

Pause for thirty seconds. If you sense Gabriel around you, continue with your request. If you feel nothing at all, repeat the request. Do this up to three times.

If you experience nothing at all, return to the list of things you are grateful for. Again, visualize them as clearly as you can. Once you have done this, ask Gabriel to come to you. This time, explain your problem or difficulty, after making the request.

Wait for thirty seconds. Hopefully, you will sense Gabriel's presence in that time. If not, repeat your request. There is no need to feel upset or concerned if Gabriel does not come to your aid immediately. You have told her what the problem is, and the answer will come to you when you least expect it. I find the most frequent time for a response is when I wake up the next morning, and find the answer has miraculously appeared in my mind.

Whether or not Gabriel has appeared, the ritual finishes in the same way. First, thank Gabriel for her help, support, and guidance. Thank her for being part of the same divine source that provided the world with all the things you were giving thanks for earlier. Go through the list of items you were grateful for again, take three deep breaths, and open your eyes.

Body, Mind, and Soul Ritual

This ritual allows you to combine and focus your body, mind, and soul. When all aspects of your being are concentrated on the same goal, you create a powerful magnet that draws to you whatever it is you desire. Naturally, for the purposes of this exercise, we are performing the ritual to contact Gabriel.

Bathe and change into fresh, clean, loose-fitting clothes. Make sure that you will not be disturbed for an hour or so. In practice, the ritual usually takes twenty to thirty minutes, but it is better to allow double that time to ensure that you will not be interrupted.

Sit down in a comfortable chair. Close your eyes, and focus on your physical body. Become aware of your breathing, and the air moving in and out of your lungs. Think about your heart and how it pumps the blood throughout your body. Think about the different organs of your body and how they perform their various functions. Think about the wonderful machinery of your spine and entire skeletal system. Become aware of any other feelings or sensations in your body.

Now think about your mind, and your ability to create thoughts and ideas. Think about the unlimited capacity of your brain. It has been estimated that you could learn something new every second of your life, and come nowhere near to filling up your brain. The potential of your mind is limitless.

Next, think of your soul, the universal life force inside every single cell in your body. Think of how you are a vital, integral part of the godhead. Whether you know it or not, you are alive at this moment for some important cosmic purpose.

Once you have done this, think about your incredible physical body, your limitless brain, and your connection to divine intelligence through your soul. Every other person on the planet has these same qualities, of course, but you are unique. There has never, in the history of mankind, been another person exactly like you. You are a miracle.

When you feel ready, picture yourself in your imagination. Focus on the area of your heart, and visualize your physical body compressing inward until it is all inside your heart. Picture your heart, and imagine your mind moving inside it. Visualize your soul, and again see it inside your heart. You are no longer a body, mind, and soul, as all three are now one. Picture this clearly in your mind. Use your imagination to make it as vivid as possible.

Now it is time to talk to Gabriel. Silently say to yourself something along these lines: "Hello Gabriel. I need your purification and guidance. Please come to my aid. I need your powers of inspiration and prophecy. Please help."

Keep thinking thoughts along these lines until you feel Gabriel has arrived. You will be in no doubt that Gabriel has come to you. You may sense a slight change in the temperature of the room. You might feel a quickening of your heart. You may simply have a strong sense of knowing that she is there. Once Gabriel has arrived, tell her what you need. Explain the whole situation, with as much detail as possible, so that Gabriel will know why her help is necessary. Gabriel might ask you a series of questions. On the other hand, she might listen quietly while you explain the situation. Of course, Gabriel will be familiar with the problem, even before she arrives, but it is necessary for you to explain the situation to her, as this helps clarify the situation in your own mind.

Once the conversation is over, thank Gabriel for coming to your aid, and say goodbye, confident that she will do everything necessary to help you resolve your difficulty.

Again, visualize every aspect of your being inside your heart. Gradually expand your physical body until you can see yourself, in your mind's eye, exactly the way you are. Become aware of your mind and allow it to expand into your brain. Feel your soul moving into every cell of your body. Give thanks to the infinite intelligence for all your talents and abilities, for your magnificent body, creative brain, and life-giving soul.

Take a few deep breaths, and open your eyes. Stretch, and think about the experience for a minute or two before carrying on with your day.

Evening Prayer Ritual

This ritual uses a traditional Jewish prayer that asks the four archangels for protection during the night. As a bonus, it also involves the Shekinah, sometimes known as the liberating angel. The Jewish Tree of Life has twelve arch-angels. Metatron and the Shekinah occupy the very top position, known as the Crown. Metatron is a strong, mas-culine energy, while the Shekinah balances this with a gen-tler, feminine energy. It is this loving, caring energy that the Shekinah supplies for additional protection through the nighttime hours.

When you are tucked up in bed, and have turned off the light, say this prayer to yourself:

"May Michael stay on my right side, Gabriel stay on my left side, Raphael stay behind me, Uriel stay in front of me, and above my head allow the divine light of the Shekinah to stay with me."

Say this prayer slowly and deliberately. Each time you mention the name of an archangel, pause and visualize his or her presence before continuing. Finally, visualize the pure white light of the Shekinah surrounding you and the archangels with love, security, and protection.

On most nights, after saying this prayer, you will fall asleep quickly and effortlessly, surrounded by the peace, tranquillity, love, and protection of the archangels. How-ever, this prayer also provides an excellent opportunity to discuss anything you wish with Gabriel, or the other arch-angels. I prefer to use this time to talk to Gabriel, as she pro-vides guidance and opens the door to visions and prophetic dreams.

The process is a simple one. Once you have finished say-ing the prayer, start by feeling the presence of the four archangels surrounding you, all bathed in the pure light of the Shekinah. Thank each archangel individually for providing you with peace, love, and protection. Thank the Shekinah for providing peace, and a close connection with the divine. Finally, tell Gabriel whatever is on your mind. You might like to roll over so that you are facing left. You might simply turn your head slightly to the left, or perhaps allow the presence of Gabriel to become slightly more apparent before starting. It makes no difference what you do, as Gabriel will instantly know that you are talking to her.

Pause every now and again to allow Gabriel to respond. You might hear words, or perhaps feel a sense of warmth or peace passing over you. Continue the conversation until you have covered everything that is on your mind. Thank Gabriel for listening and acting on your behalf. Take a slow deep breath. As you exhale, become aware of all five archangels around you. You should fall asleep almost immediately.

Usually, when I wake up the next morning after speaking with Gabriel in this way, I have plenty of energy, and my mind is full of productive ideas that I can hardly wait to put into action.

Immediate Access Ritual

There will be occasions when you need Gabriel's advice instantly. I had a minor experience like this a few weeks ago. It was a wet, windy evening and I was driving to give a talk to a group of Rotarians. It was a new part of the city and I became hopelessly lost. All of the streets I came across were too new to appear on my road map. After driving around in the torrential rain for twenty minutes, I finally did what I should have done in the first place. I stopped the car, and asked Gabriel for guidance. The instructions I received took me in a different direction to the one I had thought, but within five minutes I was parked outside the meeting venue, and walked in just as the meeting began.

When you need Gabriel's help urgently, all you need do is say, preferably out loud: "Gabriel, I need you. I need you now." You will find that Gabriel will appear instantly to offer help. Naturally, this should only be done when the need is urgent.

You now have several methods of contacting Gabriel. Experiment with them all and decide which ones you like best. Now that you know how to contact Gabriel, it is time to learn how to request assistance. That is the subject of the next chapter.

Three

HOW TO REQUEST ASSISTANCE

A S YOU know, Gabriel is willing to help you at any time. When you need help, contact Gabriel using one of the methods in the previous chapter, and then tell her exactly what you need. Once you have asked Gabriel for assistance in this way you can relax, confident that the problem is being worked on.

However, much of the time you will probably want Gabriel to help you gain spiritual insights, find your true path in life, or provide purification. You will need to create specific rituals for each of these.

To start with, it is helpful to know your personal approach to different situations. Do you work more with logic, or do you prefer to act on your feelings? Are you better at starting than finishing? Do you work well on your own, or do you need other people around you? Fortunately, it is a simple matter to determine how you think and act by using the letters in your full name at birth. This process, known as the *Temperament*, or the *Planes of Expression*, is a small part of the ancient art of numerology.

Here is the Temperament chart:

	Mental	Physical	Emotional	Intuitional
Starter	A	E	ORIZ	K
Worker	HJNP	W	BSTX	FQUY
Finisher	GL	DM		CV

Insert the letters that appear in your full name at birth under the same letters in the chart, and then add up each row, both horizontally and vertically. Here is William Shakespeare's temperament chart:

	Mental	Physical	Emotional	Intuitional	
Starter	A	E	ORIZ	K	
	AAA	EEE	RII	K	=10
Worker	HJNP	W	BSTX	FQUY	
	HP	W	SS		= 5
Finisher	GL	DM		CV	
	LL	M			= 3
	7	5	5	1	

Looking at William Shakespeare's chart, we can see that on the horizontal rows he had ten letters in the starter col-

umn, five in the worker column, and three in the finisher
column. This shows that Shakespeare was better at starting
things than he was at finishing them. He probably became
very excited with new ideas, but then had to force himself
to finish them.

Starters are enthusiastic, innovative, creative, and
inspirational.

Workers follow through on what they have started. They
are also good at following through other people's ideas.
They sometimes waver between being starters and finishers.

Finishers enjoy details and achieve enormous pleasure
when they complete projects. They are frequently stubborn.

I have an entrepreneurial friend who has started at least
twenty new businesses in the same number of years. As
soon as they are established and making a profit, he sells
them. He is a starter, not a finisher. However, the people
who buy these businesses from him are usually finishers,
and they enjoy taking over an existing corporation and
making it work efficiently and successfully. They would not
be interested in taking the risks of starting up something
new, but they can see the potential in steadily building up
an existing business.

On the vertical rows, Shakespeare has seven numbers in
the mental row, five each in the physical and emotional
rows, and one in the intuition row. Shakespeare worked
best with his mind.

When the mental row is the highest vertical column, the
person uses logic and reason more than the other qualities.

When the physical row is the highest vertical column the
person works best with concrete facts. He or she likes to

touch and feel the project. If it is physically demanding, so much the better.

When the emotional row is the highest vertical column, the person is ruled by his or her emotions. He or she can empathize, imagine, feel, and sense. This person is ruled by his or her heart.

When the intuitional row is the highest vertical row the person relies mainly on feelings and intuition. He or she tends to be impractical, and may be considered a dreamer by others. It is rare to find someone with more letters in the intuitional row than in the mind, physical, or emotional rows.

Remember that no plane is better than any other. Someone who relies primarily on his or her emotions, rather than logic, is not better or worse than the person who relies entirely on logic. It is simply a different way of looking at life. Also, the fact that someone has, say, mental as their highest rating, and intuitional as the lowest, does not mean that he or she does not rely on intuition at times. This person may be extremely intuitive, but would have to slow down his or her logical brain before using it, as under normal circumstances logic would take precedence.

You may, as Shakespeare did, have two or more columns with the same totals. (His physical and emotional rows both total five.) This means that you can make good use of the qualities of both rows.

Finally, look at the qualities of your highest vertical and horizontal rows. Shakespeare was a mental starter. He was well suited to his occupation. He was able to come up with good ideas for his plays, and probably wrote them extremely quickly, so that they could be finished before he lost interest in the project.

Again, no combination of the vertical and horizontal rows is better than any other. They simply denote different ways of thinking and acting. Someone who is an emotional starter would be quite different from someone who is a physical finisher, and they would probably choose completely different career paths. If they were both doing the same job, their approach to it and their methods of resolving problems would be quite different.

Their approach would still be quite different even if they shared one quality. An intuitive starter would be noticeably different from an intuitive finisher, as would a mental worker and an emotional worker.

Now that you know your particular way of looking at things, you can use it when you ask Gabriel for assistance.

Mental Starter

If you are a mental starter your approach is likely to be direct. If you want something, you want it now. Consequently, when asking for help, you might want to ask Gabriel for patience, as well.

Mental Worker

If you are a mental worker you will probably prefer to contact Gabriel outdoors. Ask Gabriel to help you work on the details.

Mental Finisher

If you are a mental finisher you will have a clear idea of what you want, and will be prepared to do whatever is necessary to achieve it. You are likely to ask Gabriel for help only as a last resort.

Physical Starter

If you are a physical starter you will not want to waste any time. You want to be actively involved in any solution in which you find yourself. However, you might want to ask Gabriel for patience, and to help you hang on to money once you have it.

Physical Worker

This is an unusual combination. If you are a physical worker you are likely to be impulsive and suffer from feelings of self-doubt. Ask Gabriel for patience, confidence, and caution.

Physical Finisher

If you are a physical finisher you will be realistic, responsible, and concerned about right and wrong. You may need to learn how to relax. Ask Gabriel to help you express your emotions.

Emotional Starter

If you are an emotional starter you are likely to feel things intensely. You have a drive to succeed. You have a strong creative potential. Ask Gabriel to help you relax and unwind.

Emotional Worker

If you are an emotional worker you are likely to be too self-effacing and modest. You are likely to be nervous and find it hard to let go of things that have outworn their use. Ask Gabriel for confidence, and the ability to say "no" to the excessive demands of others.

Emotional Finisher

This is another unusual combination. If you are an emotional finisher you are likely to be a worrier and a perfectionist. Ask Gabriel to help you become more outgoing and assertive.

Intuitional Starter

If you are an intuitional starter you find it hard to achieve balance in your life. You have a strong sex appeal. Ask Gabriel to help you achieve moderation in all things.

Intuitional Worker

If you are an intuitional worker you find it hard to handle responsibility and may seek escape in a variety of ways. Ask Gabriel to help you nurture yourself, and to develop mentally as well as intuitively.

Intuitional Finisher

If you are an intuitional finisher you have the potential to achieve great things as long as you apply yourself. You are likely to express yourself well. Ask Gabriel to help you set worthwhile goals for yourself.

No one approach is better than another. Fortunately, we are all different, and the approach that is perfect for you might not be as effective for someone else in your family, as their approach to life will be slightly different from yours.

How to Approach Gabriel for Spiritual Insights

People frequently say that we are spiritual beings, experiencing a physical incarnation. This is fine in theory, but many people who are aware of their spiritual side still find it hard to provide the necessary time and energy to develop it further. Everyday life is difficult enough for most people, anyway, without the added pressure of trying to develop the spiritual side of their natures. It is easy to get bogged down in the daily routine, and many people find that a large part of their life is over before they start to work on their spiritual side.

Fortunately, Gabriel can simplify the process. Once you start making regular contact with her, your desire for further knowledge and insight will grow automatically. You can ask her questions about anything.

If your spiritual vision seems to be blocked, ask her how this has occurred, and what you can do to resolve it. If you have doubts about your faith, ask Gabriel to bolster your belief. Ask Gabriel for inspirational messages to guide and help you as you develop the spiritual side of your nature. Gabriel will be a willing partner in this process, and your growth will be a joy to behold as you continue to grow and develop spiritually all the way through this incarnation.

Joshua's parents were Rationalists, and he was brought up as an atheist. He gave little thought to spiritual matters until his wife almost died of cancer. This experience caused him to reassess his own life, and to his surprise, he became extremely interested in spirituality as a way to help him understand his purpose in life. Eventually, he was introduced to the archangels, and began asking Gabriel for advice on a number of matters that were occurring in his life. One day, his life changed forever when he asked Gabriel which church he and his wife should attend. Gabriel recommended a small church on the other side of town. It seemed silly to drive all that way for a church service, and it took Joshua and his wife a few weeks before they went for the first time. The congregation appeared to be waiting for them, and they received a wonderful welcome. Now, two years later, Joshua is a lay preacher at the church, and his wife is heavily involved with the Sunday School. Thanks to Gabriel, they are both developing spiritually in the way that is right for them.

Interestingly, Anabelle, a distant relative of mine, was guided by Gabriel in a totally different direction. She began questioning her way of life after a disastrous relationship. She was already familiar with the archangels, and used Gabriel for guidance as she started to get her life back in order. She thought that she would be happy again, once she was inside a good relationship, and she was fortunate in finding a good new partner extremely quickly. However, she felt that something was missing. In her conversations with Gabriel, Anabelle discovered that the spiritual side of her life was almost nonexistent. She experimented with a number of traditions, and eventually, with the help of Gabriel, became a pagan. Some of her friends were alarmed at this change of direction, but she knew she had found the right path for her. Eventually, she was able to demonstrate to her friends that this was her particular path to spiritual growth.

How to Ask Gabriel for Help
In Finding Your True Path

Most people have doubts, every now and then, about whether or not they are following the right path through life. Fortunately, Gabriel can help you determine if you are learning the lessons that are most beneficial for the development of your soul. If, for some reason, you have strayed from the right path, Gabriel will be more than willing to help you find the correct path for you. Gabriel will be delighted to provide guidance and direction, as you cannot fulfill your life's purpose until you are on the right track.

In your conversations with Gabriel, ask her if you are on the right track. If you are, ask her for insights that will help you progress more quickly. If you are not on the right path, ask for help to get you back where you belong. If life seems purposeless and empty, the chances are high that you have strayed away from your correct path.

One of my friends always knew what he should be doing, but fought it, because of family disapproval. His father was a judge and wanted him to follow a legal career. However, Liam had always wanted to be an artist. As a child, everyone loved the artwork he produced, but his parents were furious when he announced that he wanted to make a career of it. Consequently, he studied law and became a mediocre lawyer. He made a good living, but hated every moment of it. Not surprisingly, in his early thirties, he had a complete physical and mental breakdown. This forced him to take a good look at his life and see what he was doing to himself. In the process, Liam discovered the angelic kingdom and began developing spiritually. As a result of this, he decided to change careers and become an artist. Even then he was not prepared to tell his parents what he intended doing. He told them he was taking a year off to fully recover.

Liam and his wife moved to a small seaside cottage where he began painting again. It took several months before he sold anything. However, he was not concerned about this, as Gabriel had confirmed that he was finally doing what he was put on this earth to achieve. By the end of twelve months, he was making a modest income from his art, and decided to carry on with this new career. He is still making a mere fraction of the money he made as an attorney, but looks years younger than he did before, and feels totally fulfilled and happy for the first time in his adult life.

How to Ask Gabriel for Purification

Purification is something everyone needs at some stage. You will need physical purification if, for instance, your body is full of toxins. You will need mental purification if your mind is full of impure or negative thoughts. If you have been molested, or abused in any other way, you might need purification so that you can start moving forward again. If you are codependent, or have taken other people's problems on your shoulders for too long, you will need purification. Once the purification has been completed, you can make the changes in your life that need to be made so that you can start moving ahead again.

The process is extremely straightforward. In your conversations with Gabriel ask her to purify your body, mind, and spirit. You have probably heard of surrounding yourself with white light whenever you need protection. You can use this to help provide purification, also. Start by closing your eyes and mentally visualizing yourself surrounded by white light. Once you can see this clearly in your mind, picture Gabriel standing outside the white light. She is holding a large hose, exactly like the ones that fire fighters use. As you watch, she turns it on and hoses you, not with water, but with the purest white energy that you can imagine. She hoses your physical body, from the top of your head to the tips of your toes. Feel the tingling sensation as the white light thoroughly cleanses your physical body. Once your physical body has been purified, visualize her starting again, but this time she purifies your mental body with that pure white light. Again, she washes you from head to toe with the energy from the hose. Once that has been completed, picture her purifying your spiritual body with the incredible healing energy of white light. Again, this is done by sending the pure white light from the hose to every part of your spiritual body. Finally, see Gabriel turn off the hose. Thank her, and stand in the white light that surrounds you for as long as possible. When you feel ready, carry on with your day. Repeat at least once a day, until you feel totally restored. Even then, it would be helpful to perform this ritual at least once a week to eliminate any potential problems before they start.

One of my students had been beaten up and raped a couple of years before attending my psychic development classes. She had tried everything she could think of to get her life back to the way it had been before the attack, but still felt dirty in body, mind, and soul. Seeing her abuser sentenced to a lengthy prison term helped her temporarily, but she soon began feeling unclean again. She started hosing herself twice every day, and experienced immediate results. However, it still took several months before she felt that her life was as good as it had been before the attack. Although it took time, her recovery shows just how beneficial and healing this particular exercise is.

How to Ask Gabriel for Clarity

Archangel Gabriel will always be happy to bring you messages. She did this for Joan of Arc, the Virgin Mary, and many other people throughout history. There is no reason why she will not do the same for you. However, you may need to ask her to do this. The first time many people ask Gabriel for help in this way is when they experience a strange dream that they are unable to interpret. Naturally, Gabriel will be willing to assist.

You may feel that your intuition has somehow become blocked. One man told me that he felt as if his third eye had closed down. Others have described it as an unwillingness to accept any perceptions that came through. Whatever the cause, Gabriel will be happy to restore and enhance your intuition.

If you have important decisions to make, or are unsure as to your future direction, ask Gabriel to provide you with prophetic visions of the future. By doing this, you have an opportunity to see what the future will be like. If you are unhappy with the future that the visions reveal, you can ask Gabriel to help you make changes so that the future will become one that you will be happy with.

All of these requests can be made in the course of a conversation with Gabriel. Naturally, you can create a formal ritual, if you wish. I have done both in the past, and have found each equally helpful. However, if you are experiencing a lack of intuitive insights, or are reluctant to accept any that do come through, it is a good idea to set aside a session purely to resolve this.

Do not eat for at least two hours before the session. Drink water if you feel thirsty during this time. You want your mind to be clear and alert while you have this conversation.

Sit down somewhere where you will not be disturbed. Make sure that you are as comfortable as possible. Once you have contacted Gabriel, tell her about your concerns. Tell her that your intuition is not working as well as it should. You may even know the reason for this. If so, tell Gabriel all about it.

Many years ago, I met a man who had had several dreams about meeting a certain woman. When he finally met her in real life, the love affair that he thought would follow did not happen. In fact, the woman disliked him intensely. The man was so traumatized by this that he resolved never to accept anything that his dreams told him ever again. Not surprisingly, his subconscious mind made this a reality. Unfortunately, it went too far and his subconscious mind prevented him from receiving any intuitive insights at all. Once he realized what he had done to himself, he had a conversation with Gabriel about it, and the difficulty was resolved. This example shows that we need to be careful what we ask for, as the results can sometimes be much more profound and far-reaching than intended.

You need to listen intently while performing this ritual. You are doing it to restore or enhance your intuition. Consequently, you need to be extremely aware of any insights that do come through to you. Usually, one session will be all that is required. However, you might want to perform it several times to ensure that your intuition has been fully restored.

Sending a Letter to Gabriel

You will find it helpful to send letters to Gabriel. Sometimes it can be easier to express your thoughts with words on paper, rather than expressing them in thoughts or lengthy speeches. Forget formal, business-type letters. Your letters to Gabriel can be as casual as you wish. I always start my letters with "Dear Gabriel," and finish by expressing my love to her. However, the actual content of the letter varies enormously, depending on my reason for writing.

Sometimes I will write a letter of thanks to Gabriel, telling her how much I appreciate all her efforts on my behalf. On other occasions, I may need help of some sort, and naturally these letters are related to my areas of concern. Every now and again, I am not entirely sure what I want to write about, and these letters are inclined to ramble a bit as I gradually work out why I felt impelled to write at that particular time.

Whenever possible, I use good quality stationery and a fountain pen. However, if these are not available I will write the letter on any piece of paper that happens to be close at hand. Once the letter is finished, I sign it and then seal it in an envelope.

The next step is to send this letter to Gabriel. You can do this by finding a private space, preferably outdoors, and burning the envelope, while at the same time offering thanks to Gabriel. Although I do send the letter this way when my time is limited, I prefer to create a small ritual, during which I formally send the letter to Gabriel.

I use a single, white candle which I place on my altar. An altar is simply a convenient place to perform any spiritual or magical activities. I have a table that is dedicated to this purpose. However, any surface will do, as long as it is clean, and you regard it with respect. Many people use part of the kitchen table. As any surface can act as an impromptu altar, you do not need to hunt around for the right surface.

I place the candle near the back of the altar, and position the letter in front of it. I sit or kneel directly in front of it. I light the candle, and then close my eyes and invoke the archangels. When I feel their presence, I thank them for their help, guidance, and protection. I then pick up the letter with both hands and symbolically offer it to Gabriel. I then burn it in the candle flame while thanking Gabriel for her help, not only with my immediate concern, but for everything she has done for me. Once this is done, I pause for a minute or two, enjoying being in the company of the archangels. Finally, I thank them, put out the candle, and carry on with my day.

If you experiment with this, you will be delighted to discover that this ritual immediately frees you from all your cares and worries. You will be able to carry on with your life, feeling rejuvenated and free of the huge burden of problems that you had been carrying for so long.

Gabriel is prepared to offer help and guidance whenever you wish. All you need to do is ask. It is a wonderful feeling to know that you can call on Gabriel whenever you have a problem that appears insurmountable. However, you will also find it useful to contact Gabriel for a few minutes every day. That is the subject of the next chapter.

Four

HOW TO CONTACT GABRIEL EVERY DAY

IT IS WONDERFUL to have Gabriel as a caring friend, someone who is willing to do everything she possibly can to help you. Because of this, you will probably want to contact her every day. Obviously, you will not want to make a nuisance of yourself, but there is no reason why you should not perform a brief ritual every day to contact Gabriel, and to thank her for looking after you.

You can do this by using any of the methods in chapter two. However, I prefer to perform a special ritual that is dedicated solely to thanking Gabriel. I make no requests or petitions while performing this. The whole point of it is to thank Gabriel sincerely for everything she does. I want her to receive my thanks, and to know how grateful I am, but I do not want to pester her with requests and demands on a daily basis.

In practice, I might request Gabriel's help two or three times in a single month, and then not need her help for the next three or four. It is best to work on solving your own problems, and call on the archangels only when you feel it is necessary.

Obviously, whenever you are contacting Gabriel, you will need a suitable space and enough time to complete the communication. Theoretically, any space would suffice, but it is a good idea to use the same place every time, if possible. Whenever possible, I try to bathe beforehand as well, and then change into fresh clothes. As you know, it is helpful to start this way whenever you perform a ritual. However, as you will see, this ritual is so quick and easy to do that you can perform it even while sitting at a desk at work.

Ritual of Thanks

There are four stages to the ritual:

1. Creating the *cosmic mudra*

2. Abdominal breathing

3. Contacting Gabriel

4. Expressing your thanks

It is a good idea to spend a few minutes thinking about Gabriel and what she does for you before starting the ritual. As I do this, I feel a sense of anticipation and excitement, knowing that shortly I will be thanking her for her many blessings in my life. When I feel ready, I start on the ritual itself.

Creating the Cosmic Mudra

Although you can perform this ritual sitting down, I prefer to stand up for it. You start by creating the cosmic mudra with your hands. Place the edge of your right hand, palm side upward, against your lower abdomen, a few inches below your navel. This part of the abdomen is considered a seat of power and energy, and the true home of the life force, in many traditions. Theron Q. Dumont considered the solar plexus to be so important that he called it the "abdominal brain."[1] Your little finger should rest against your abdomen. Place the back of your left hand on the palm of your right hand. The knuckles of the fingers on each hand should overlap. Allow the tips of your thumbs to touch each other, and you have created the cosmic mudra.

The word "mudra" comes from the Sanskrit and means "a gesture, posture, or seal." A mudra is a symbolic gesture made by the hands and fingers. You may wonder what the word "seal" means in the definition of mudra. When you touch your thumbs together, you effectively create a seal, closing off the mudra. This means that you have physically and symbolically closed off and sealed the area where the ritual is to take place.

Mudras are used extensively in Indian ritual and dance, and each movement has a specific meaning. When used in a ritual, the precise formation made by the hands stimulates, strengthens, and reinforces the spiritual experience. In a sense, mudras are a sign language that causes changes in our physical, mental, and spiritual bodies. Statues of Buddha frequently depict mudras. You may have seen him with his right hand at shoulder height, which means "there is no need to fear," or with his right hand resting in the palm of his left hand, which indicates meditation. Mudras can be used to express almost anything. When you shake your fist at someone, you are creating a mudra that shows your anger. When you place your hands together to make a prayer, you are creating a mudra of piety.

You will find that standing or sitting with your hands forming the cosmic mudra is restful and relaxing.

Abdominal Breathing

The next stage is to focus on your breathing. Breathe through your nose, and feel the air as it enters your nostrils. Allow the inhalation to move down to your abdomen. When you breathe abdominally, your abdomen moves in and out with each breath, while your chest stays almost still. You will feel your abdomen expand against the little finger of your right hand as you inhale, and then contract again as you exhale.

Many people find abdominal breathing difficult. If this is the case, start by breathing normally. Notice the regular rhythm of your breathing. After several breaths, hold your inhalation instead of releasing it. Push your solar plexus out, and then exhale while deliberately drawing in your stomach muscles. Repeat this several times, until you are breathing abdominally without any effort. If you practice breathing abdominally whenever you perform this ritual, you will suddenly find that you have the knack, and will not need to consciously think of it again.

When performing the ritual, take several slow, deep breaths, holding each breath for a few moments before exhaling. You will find that the combination of the mudra and the abdominal breathing allows you to briefly escape all the cares of the day, even if you are surrounded by others at the time.

Contacting Gabriel

When you feel ready, ask Gabriel to join you. After you have practiced this ritual a number of times, you will probably find that simply saying: "Hello, Gabriel" to yourself is all that is required. However, when you first start practicing this daily ritual you may find it better to ask Gabriel to join you, and then wait until you sense her presence. If nothing happens within a minute, focus on your breathing for several inhalations, and then invite Gabriel once again to join you. If you still have no response, separate your hands and shake them vigorously by your sides. Drink some water and then start the ritual again.

In practice, you will find it rare for Gabriel to not appear instantly. You may have been overly anxious for her to come. You may have experienced an unusual amount of stress immediately before doing the ritual. You may not have been able to devote your entire attention to the ritual. Any problems of this sort will be short lived. These difficulties will cease to occur once you get into the habit of communicating with Gabriel every day.

Expressing Your Thanks

Once Gabriel is with you, express your love for her, and thank her for everything that she has done, and is doing, for you. Express your gratitude to her for always being there for you. Pause to receive an acknowledgment, and then say goodbye. Your farewell should be positive and upbeat, just as if you were saying goodbye to a close friend whom you will be seeing again in a day or two.

I finish by rubbing my hands briskly together, and then carry on with my day.

As you can see, the entire ritual can be done in under a minute, if your time is limited. I try not to rush through any ritual, preferring to spend as much time as is necessary to perform it properly. Usually, this simple ritual takes me three or four minutes. Even though this ritual may seem inconsequential, it will have a powerful effect on your life. The fact that you are in daily communication with one of the great archangels should be uplifting, and give you the confidence to tackle projects that might have seemed overwhelming before. Experiment with it, and see what effect it has on your life.

Gabriel and the Dying

This may not sound like a cheerful topic, but it can be useful to contact Gabriel when you know someone is dying, or immediately after his or her death. There are still many taboos about death, and you need to be careful when talking about angels with people who are terminally ill. However, it is possible to help them without necessarily mentioning the angelic kingdom. The best way, of course, is to be there for them. Give them all the love you can. Read to them, visit them, and support them in every way possible. Pray for them, of course, but do not try to hold them back on their path of spiritual evolution.

Gabriel bridges the gap between this world and the next, and will be happy to guide and assist the soul in the afterlife. Naturally, Azrael, the angel of death, will be there, too. He appears automatically at the time of death to take the person on the next stage of their journey. He will be delighted to have Gabriel accompany the soul as it familiarizes itself with the next life.

Consequently, ask Gabriel to assist your friend both before and after death. Keep your friend in your prayers for several weeks after he or she has passed over. Thank Gabriel each time you pray for the help she is providing your friend.

In the next chapter we will start exploring other ways of contacting Gabriel. The first of these is the little-known art of cord magic.

Five

CORD MAGIC

IN THE KORAN (Surah 113) mention is made of "blowers on knots." These are people who recite spells intended to harm people, while tying knots. One of these people, called Lubaid, tied eleven knots onto a piece of rope and dropped it into a well to cause the prophet Muhammad harm. In fact, Muhammad would have died if God had not sent him the vital two Surahs (112 and 113). He also sent Gabriel to teach Muhammad how to use them. The rope was retrieved and Muhammad recited the eleven verses of the Surahs over the knots. One knot untied itself at the end of each line, and at the end of the recitation, Mohammed was free of the enchantment.[1]

You are probably familiar with the Victorian term "tying the knot," which indicates that a couple are getting married. A knot still symbolizes love, union, and permanent relationships. Brahmins wear knotted cords to bind them to Brahma. Franciscan friars wear thrice-knotted cords that effectively bind them to their vows of poverty, celibacy, and obedience. If someone is "bound" to do something, he or she will certainly do it. These terms are all derived from knot magic. In fact, whenever you tie a string around a finger to help you remember something that needs to be done you are performing a form of knot magic.

Cord, or knot magic is not well known today, but it has a long history. Magical knots were found on the mummy of King Tutankhamen, showing the age of this form of magic.[2] The Knot of Isis, a knot that looked liked an ankh with folded arms, was worn by the ancient Egyptians as a protective amulet.[3] The figure-of-eight knot, made in gold, was popular at the time of the Middle Kingdom. Examples of these knots, used as anklets and bracelets, have been found in several burial sites.[4] The famous Gordian knot promised all of Asia to the person who could untie it. Alexander the Great impatiently cut the knot apart, and achieved only part of his goal. In Roman times, people were not allowed to wear knotted garments in the temple of Juno Lucina, the goddess of childbirth. This is because they believed in sympathetic magic, and a knot indicated a blockage, the last thing that was desired in a temple devoted to childbirth.[5] Fifteen hundred years later, knots were tied in men's codpieces to prevent an engaged couple from consummating the marriage until after the wedding ceremony.[6]

There are many superstitions about knots. Sailors tied knots in their shirts for protection during storms. Gamblers also tied knots in the same way to attract good luck. Even today, there are people who tie knots on their kitchen aprons for protection. Knots were also tied to catch evil spirits. Clerical collars come from this, as people thought that evil spirits could hide in priests' ties and disturb religious services.[7]

Knots have always played a role in folk magic. While tying knots people focused their attention on their problems. When they consciously added energy to their thoughts, they subconsciously attracted whatever it was they sought. If someone had a problem, for instance, he or she would tie a number of knots in a length of cord while thinking about the concern. The knots also symbolized the problem. Usually, an odd number of knots would be tied. The person would then recite some magical words while untying the knots. Part of the problem disappeared as each knot was untied, and once they had all been undone, the person was free of the problem or difficulty. Sometimes the cord would be burned afterward, especially if the problem was a major one.

However, knot magic is much more versatile than that, and can be used to establish an even closer connection with Gabriel. First of all, you need to braid a suitable cord. You will need three lengths of cords, one each of gold, silver, and white. The gold cord symbolizes God and anything masculine. Silver represents the Goddess and anything feminine. The white cord symbolizes you.

Ideally, these cords should be made from natural fibers, such as wool or silk. They should be about nine feet long.

Carefully braid the three cords together. Do not rush this. You are symbolically joining yourself (white) to the male (gold) and female (silver) aspects of the universal life force. Think about this as you braid the cords together. Consider the close, intimate connection that this braiding causes. Think how wonderful your life would be if you could remain in such a close connection with God all the time. Ask Gabriel to bless your work. When you have finished the braiding, tie a knot at each end to prevent it from unraveling.

This cord needs to be consecrated before using it for the first time. You can do this in a number of ways. If you have an altar, place it in the center and light a single white candle. Hold the candle above the cord and say out loud: "May the light of this pure candle cleanse and purify you." Make three clockwise circles over the cord with the candle, say "thank you," and snuff out the candle. Finish by saying: "I dedicate this cord to Gabriel." The cord is now ready for use. You can use a handful of rock salt in preference to the candle, if you wish. In this case, sprinkle the cord with salt as you speak, and again as you make the three circles with your hand. Another method of consecrating your cord is to stand outside in direct sunlight with the cord draped over your extended arms. Say: "May the rays of the sun cleanse and purify you." Make three clockwise circles. Say "thank you" and pause for several seconds before saying: "I dedicate you to Gabriel." Finish by tying the cord around your waist.

The finished cord is known as a cingulum, and can be worn around your waist while performing any magical or spiritual work. Put your cingulum away carefully whenever you have finished working with it. You might keep it in a special box or wrapped in a silk cloth. Treat it with love and respect. It should not be tossed carelessly to one side, or left somewhere once you have finished working with it.

The Witches' Ladder

The witches' ladder is a series of knots, usually nine, that are formed in the cingulum to create a form of rosary. With certain spells, a specific word might have to be recited a certain number of times. By sliding your fingers along the cord and over each knot, you can say the word the required number of times without worrying about keeping count.

The knots are tied in a specific order while you think about your goal, and recite a few words as each knot is tied. Until you get used to the correct order, it is a good idea to tie the knots while your cingulum is lying on a table or altar in front of you. Once you become used to the order of knots, you will be able to tie the knots while holding the cingulum between your hands. Start by tying a knot at the left-hand end of your cingulum. Tie the second knot at the right-hand end. Your cingulum now has a knot at each end. Tie the third knot in the middle. The fourth knot is tied halfway between the left-hand end and the center knot. This places it one quarter of the way along your cingulum. The fifth knot is tied halfway between this knot and the knot at the left-hand end (one eighth of the way along the cingulum from the left-hand end). You now move to the other half of the cingulum and tie the sixth knot between the knot in the center and the knot at the right-hand end. This is three-quarters of the way along your cingulum from the left. The seventh knot is tied seven-eighths of the way along the cingulum, between the knot at the three-quarters position and the knot at the right-hand end. The positions of the final two knots will be obvious at this stage, as the three-eighths and five-eighths positions, on either side of the center knot, will be the only free spaces left. Tie the eighth knot in the three-eighths position and the final knot in the five-eighths position. All of this is illustrated in the following diagram:

```
X
X                                       X
X                       X               X
X           X           X               X
X   X   X           X               X
X   X   X           X       X           X
X   X   X           X       X   X   X
X   X   X   X   X           X   X   X
X   X   X   X   X   X   X   X   X
```

Traditionally, each knot is tied as you say a rhyming couplet. Each line starts with "by knot of." If you are using knot magic to gain a closer connection with Gabriel, you might say the following words as you tie each knot:

"By knot of one, my spell's begun."
"By knot of two, Gabriel's in view."
"By knot of three, so shall it be."

"By knot of four, for ever more."
"By knot of five, may our love survive."
"By knot of six, Gabriel will fix."
"By knot of seven, my path to heaven."
"By knot of eight, together our fate."
"By knot of nine, we intertwine."

Once all the knots have been tied, and the spell recited, you will find it helpful to repeat the spell again, holding each knot in turn. Finish by saying: "Thank you, Gabriel."

Creating a witches' ladder allows you to direct all your attention and energy on the result you desire—in this case, a closer communication with Gabriel. It can be helpful to visualize yourself imbuing each knot with vibrant energy and power as you tie it. The knots then become storehouses of energy that you can make use of whenever you wish. You will feel the difference in your cingulum as soon as it is energized in this way.

Your witches' ladder can be used in a variety of ways. You can use it as a rosary, repeating the name "Gabriel" nine times as you run your fingers along your cingulum. You can wear the cingulum as a belt, either visibly, or concealed under other clothing, to keep Gabriel with you at all times. Alternatively, you might like to purify a small corner of your garden and bury the cingulum there. Some people prefer to keep their witches' ladder indoors, rather than out. This can be done by burying it in an earth-filled ceramic pot. Keep this container on your altar, or in a special place where it will not be disturbed, but where you will see it frequently.

I prefer to keep my cingulum in a box, so that I can pick it up whenever I wish. I know people who keep their cingulums in a box, covered with earth or sand. I have a special box for it, and this has gained power and energy also, as a result of holding my cingulum.

One advantage of having my cingulum handy is an interesting exercise that involves creating a witches' ladder, and then untying the knots one by one to release energy to achieve a specific goal. It is important that the knots be untied in the same order that you tied them. The first knot you tied is the first to be untied. Consequently, it is a good idea to mark the first knot in some way, just in case you cannot remember which end you tied first. You can do this by marking it with a felt marker, or you may prefer to tie something into the knot itself. A feather, twig, or short piece of thread all work well.

Let's assume that you are thinking of changing careers and want Gabriel's guidance. In this case, you create the witches' ladder while thinking of your desire to change careers. By the time you have created the ladder, the cingulum will be full of power and energy. This energy is then released into the universe slowly by untying one knot a day for nine days. Naturally, you should untie each knot slowly and solemnly, while thinking of your ultimate goal. At the moment the knot becomes undone, exhale sharply, or call out "release!" Each knot contains power, but the most important one is the ninth knot that you untie on the last day.

I usually untie all the knots while standing, rather than sitting down. Even if you sit on the first eight days, stand while untying the final knot. Spread your arms out wide once the knot has been released, and shout "thank you, Gabriel" as loudly as you can. By the time you have reached this stage, you should have a clear idea as to what you want to do regarding your request. In this example, you may have decided not to change careers, you might have new ideas about the direction you intend to move into, or you may even have found yourself a new position. No matter what the outcome is, it will be the right one for you, and you will know this, thanks to Gabriel's involvement in the entire process.

I like to untie the knots at the same time each day, but do not worry about this if it is not possible. The important part of the process is to think seriously about your desires while untying the knot. You can also use this time to speak to Gabriel about your purpose in performing this ritual.

The process of untying the knots in a witches' ladder is different if you are doing it for purification purposes. You might want to do this if, for example, you are finding it hard to recover from an illness and wish to release the toxins that are still in your body. You might be thinking negative thoughts about yourself, or others. You might feel unclean because of something that has happened to you.

In cases like these, you need to create a special witches' ladder because you will destroy it at the end of the process. All you need is a length of string or soft rope. Create a witches' ladder in the usual way, while thinking about your need for purification. Bury this ladder in earth for at least twenty-four hours before untying the first knot. Each day, as you untie a knot, call out: "Gabriel, purify my mind, body, and spirit. Make me whole." You will feel a sense of relief and release as you untie the first knot, and this feeling will increase steadily, day by day. The feeling of release is likely to be profound, and sometimes dramatic, when you untie the final knot. Do not try to hold your emotions back while untying the knots. Releasing your feelings in this way helps the entire process. Thank Gabriel for her help in purifying and restoring your soul. Finally, burn the string or rope. You are likely to feel a profound sense of peace and happiness once this has been done.

You can repeat this process as many times as necessary. Most of the time, one nine-day cycle is sufficient, but in extreme cases you may have to repeat it a number of times. One of my students who had been sexually abused as a child performed this ritual seven times before she felt clean and whole again.

Gabriel's Knot

Gabriel's knot is a single knot tied on a length of white or dark blue cord. You can either wear or carry this knot with you to ensure that Gabriel's energies stay with you at all times. In effect, the knot becomes a point of contact between you and Gabriel. If you always have it with you, you can touch or hold it whenever you need Gabriel's guidance, support, or inspiration.

Choose an attractive length of cord or rope, approximately twelve inches long. Sit down and hold the rope in your right palm. Rest the back of this hand on your left palm, while making contact with Gabriel. Once Gabriel has arrived, tell her what you intend doing with the rope. Say that you intend creating a binding knot, full of her energies, to carry with you to help you achieve whatever it is you are seeking. Ask her permission to do this. In my experience, this will always be granted, but you should always ask, rather than assuming that Gabriel will agree.

Once you have permission, close your right hand into a fist, enclosing part, or all, of the cord. Close your eyes and visualize yourself surrounded by a pure white light. Picture Gabriel in the middle of this white light, filling you and the cord with her divine energy. Hold this image for as long as you can. When it starts to fade, thank Gabriel, open your eyes and make a single knot in the center of the piece of rope. You may want to trim the ends of the rope for cosmetic reasons. This is fine, as the energy is contained in the knot itself. Attach the knot to your clothing, or carry it with you. Touch or fondle the knot whenever you feel the need for Gabriel's protective energy.

Gabriel Bag

Gabriel bags are an interesting, unusual, yet effective way of using Gabriel's energies to enhance the quality of your life. Choose a small cotton or silk bag, no larger than five inches square. Inside this place any small objects that symbolize Gabriel to you. You might choose something white or indigo, as these are Gabriel's colors. Crystals make a good choice, and can enhance your communication with Gabriel. Blue calcite, iolite, lapis lazuli, and Tanzanite all relate well with Gabriel's energies. You might choose to write a short letter to Gabriel and place that in the bag. One of my students cut a heart shape out of cardboard and wrote Gabriel's name on it. It makes no difference what item or items you choose, just as long as there is some association between them and Gabriel.

You now need to tie the bag shut, and this is where the knot magic comes in. You might braid colored cord together to create a miniature cingulum. Alternatively, a single piece of white or indigo cord will also work well. Start by winding the center of the cord around the top of the bag three times, and then tie three knots. Repeat this twice more, so that you end up with nine knots to keep the bag closed.

The final stage in the process is to ask Gabriel to bless the bag. Hold the bag in your right hand, and rest the back of this hand on your left palm. Sit down comfortably and ask Gabriel to join you. When she arrives, thank her for her love and devotion, and then ask her to bless your Gabriel bag. Tell her that you intend to carry it with you to ensure that her energies are with you at all times. When you feel her blessing, thank her, and then hold the bag between your cupped hands. Feel your personal energy flowing from your palms into the bag to join the energy that Gabriel has already placed there.

The bag is now ready to be used as a protective amulet. Whenever you need guidance, vision, inspiration, or purity, hold the bag between your cupped hands and allow the energy from it to flow into every part of your body.

Many people like to scent their bag in some way. Most of the time, this will make the bag more appealing and inviting to you. As a bonus, the right choice of scent will also enable you and your Gabriel bag to enjoy an even closer connection with Gabriel. That is the subject of the next chapter.

Six

GABRIEL, PERFUMES, AND SCENTS

THROUGHOUT history, priests, chemists, and magicians have created special essences for a variety of purposes. In the Book of Exodus, God gave Moses instructions on how to make an anointing oil and a special perfume to use when giving praise to God (Exodus 30: 23–38). In the same chapter, Aaron was told to burn a sweet incense every morning as an offering to God (Exodus 30: 7–9). In the Book of Revelation, an angel burned incense before the trumpets sounded.

The ancient Egyptians were also aware that perfumes and incense can reach aspects of consciousness that can not be accessed any other way. The god Ra was believed to draw souls up to the Halls of Amenti, the home of the gods, on the sweet smoke of incense. The manufacture of incense was a ritual in itself, and sacred books were read while it was prepared in the temples. Egyptian doctors used incense to fumigate and cleanse the rooms of their patients. Apparently, the fragrance of incense could still be detected in the tomb of Tutankhamen three thousand years after it was prepared.[1] It is believed that Cleopatra used her knowledge of incense, perfume, and oils to ensnare her lovers. She did this by soaking her gowns in a perfume that her lovers could not resist.[2]

In India, the Hindus make incense from sweet-smelling woods. They also use perfumed water as an offering to the gods. People in Tibet place incense in their amulet boxes to ward off negative spirits. The Chinese still make regular use of joss sticks on ceremonial occasions.

Angels frequently have a special, delicate perfume of their own. Many people have told me that they became aware of a magnificent, otherworldly scent shortly before an angel appeared to them. This aroma would often linger in the room for an hour or more after the angel departed.

Consequently, sachets, potpourri, special oils, and perfumes have always been used as offerings to the divine, and are an extremely effective way of drawing angels to you. In addition to this, the special aromas will increase your receptiveness and make you more aware of the angelic kingdom.

Although our sense of smell is not as great as that of many other animals, we have more highly developed brains that can process smells accurately and precisely. Although we are not consciously aware of it, humans can actually smell other people's emotional states, levels of health and well-being, and degree of sensuality.[3]

Incense

Incense has been used for thousands of years. All sorts of materials have been experimented with in attempts to enhance the magical experience. Today, most incense is made from herbs. You can buy loose incense, but stick or cone incense is more convenient, safer, and easier to use.

You can make your own incense, if you wish, and there are many books that will teach you how to do it.[4] One of the advantages of making your own incense, essential oils, or perfumes is that you can imbue your feelings and desires into every step of the process. Always work in a well-ventilated area, and take every precaution possible. Read the instructions carefully. Many people find they get headaches after working with scents for any length of time. To avoid these, take frequent breaks outdoors, and enjoy some fresh air.

If you decide to buy incense, in preference to making it, check out church supply stores, as well as new age and occult shops.

Any scent that appeals to you can be used to either contact Gabriel or to add strength and power to any ritual involving you and Gabriel. However, there are many scents that specifically relate to Gabriel, and you should use these if you do not have a strong favorite personal scent.

The scents you use are related to your purpose in contacting Gabriel.

If you are seeking guidance you should use: acacia, ambretta, champaca, fern, ginger, hawthorn, lilac, lily, neroli, patchouli, rose, sage, sweet pea, and tolu oil.

If you are seeking purification you should use: ambretta, calamus oil, iris, mint, myrtle, reseda grass, thyme, wallflower, and wintergreen.

If you need help to eliminate doubts and fears, use: ambretta, angelica, bergamot, carnation, citronella, lemon balm, lime, melissa, mimosa, myrtle, oregano, pimento, and salvia sclareci. The following are useful for creating peace of mind: aloe, chamomile, gardenia, lavender, myrtle, and violet.

If you wish to enhance your powers of vision, prophecy and insight, use: acacia, cyclamen, heliotrope, jonquil, lily, neroli, rue, tolu oil, and tuberose.

If you are specifically interested in developing your psychic powers, use: bay laurel, cinnamon, eyebright, hazel, hyssop, lavender, marigold, nutmeg, oak, rose, thyme, wormwood, and yarrow.

If you feel the need for protection use: aloe, anise, Balm of Gilead, basil, caraway, chamomile, clove, dragon's blood, garlic, hawthorn, hyssop, ivy, mandrake, marjoram, meadow sweet, mistletoe, onion, periwinkle, rosemary, rowan, sage, St. John's wort, sandalwood, witch hazel, and wormwood.

Astrologically, the moon is under the angelic rulership of Gabriel. The incenses that relate to the moon are convolvulus, camphor, jasmine, Madonna lilies, narcissi, patchouli, and poppy. With the exception of poppy, a narcotic, these herbs create drowsiness, which explains their attribution to the moon, the planet associated with dreams and intuition.

Essential Oils

Essential oils are fragrances that are created by plants. In some cases, one plant can provide a number of different oils. Neroli, for instance, comes from the flowers of an orange tree, petitgrain comes from the leaves of the same plant, and orange comes from the fruit.

Like everything else, you get what you pay for. It is possible to buy synthetic essential oils, but you will not receive the same benefits from them that you will gain from genuine essential oils. When you consider that it can take forty roses to produce a single drop of rose essential oil, you will understand why they are expensive. Ensure that you purchase good quality oils that have an expiration date on the label and are packed in dark glass bottles to protect and preserve the oils.

Essential oils can be used in a variety of ways. I find it helpful to add a few drops of essential oil to a saucer of boiling water on my altar. Obviously, this saucer must be placed somewhere where it will not be bumped or upset. It is even better to use a diffuser that is heated by a candle. Put three teaspoons of cold water into the bowl and add a few drops of an essential oil before lighting the candle. The aroma will be almost undetectable at first, but will gradually fill the room.

Another effective method is to sprinkle a few drops of essential oil on pillows and cushions in your sacred space. You can encourage Gabriel to come to you in your dreams by adding a couple of drops of essential oil to your pillow before going to bed.

Adding a few drops of an essential oil to an incense stick adds extra power to whatever ritual you are performing.

There are a huge number of essential oils available. They are frequently used to help cure physical problems, but the effect they have on our emotional and spiritual sides is far more important, as they can help us contact the angelic kingdom, and also treat the emotional causes behind many physical problems.

I first became aware of the incredible power of essential oils when a member of a breakfast club I belong to began experimenting with them. At each meeting she would use a different oil, without telling us what effect it would have on us. Invariably, the whole tone of the meeting was determined by the oil she chose. When she used jasmine, for instance, the meetings were lively and full of fun. However, when she used sandalwood we were quieter and more introspective.

There are a number of oils that can be used to help make contact with Gabriel. Lavender is a good choice if you are seeking purification. It is a nurturing oil that allows you to banish doubts and fears and start over again. Pine increases your self-worth, and is another good choice if you are seeking purification. German chamomile allows you to let go of the past, so that you can start moving forward again. Patchouli creates balance, harmony, and wholeness. When all sides of your makeup are in balance, you can achieve anything you set your mind on. If you want guidance from Gabriel, try black pepper. It helps you achieve focus and move forward in the right direction. Peppermint is a good choice if you want help with your vision and inspiration. Rosewood will help you develop the psychic, intuitive side of your makeup. Sandalwood provides protection from the negativity of others. Frankincense also provides protection, while keeping you focused on whatever your goals may be. It ensures that you grow in knowledge and wisdom. Tea Tree allows you to accept yourself as you are, and also helps you understand the motivations of others. Ylang Ylang brings peace, tranquillity, and calm. It eliminates negative emotions, and nurtures the feminine side of our natures.

Potpourri

Our grandparents made regular use of potpourri to freshen and sweeten the environment. It is possible to obtain special potpourri bowls, which have lids containing several small holes to allow the fragrance out. However, an open ceramic or pottery bowl is all that is necessary. Mix the herbs that appeal to you, place them in the container, and allow the scent to subtly change the feel of the room.

Sachets

A sachet is a cloth bag filled with herbs or other fragrances. In a sense, it is a closed, portable potpourri. It is usually used to scent clothing while it is being stored. However, sachets can also be used to strengthen the energies of any magical tools you may have. They can also be carried, worn around the neck, or placed inside your pillow. Keeping one in your car ensures that you will enjoy the benefits everywhere you go. A Gabriel bag is a form of sachet.

Sachet bags can be made from any type of cloth. Muslin is a good choice. The bag should be large enough to hold several tablespoons of herbs. You can use any aromatic herbs you wish. Choose these, either by referring to specialist books to choose the right herbs for your particular goal, or by using your intuition. Vervain is a good choice for any spiritual or magical purpose.

Sachet bags should be replaced every so often. Once a year is about the right length of time if they are being used to purify or consecrate clothing, tools, or a sacred space. However, if you are wearing or carrying the sachet with you it should be replaced every three to four months.

Baths

Herbal baths are a pleasant way to gain the qualities that the herbs provide. A herbal bath can provide protection, enhance intuition, and make it easier for you to attract to you whatever it is that you desire. Bath sachets are easily made by mixing the desired herbs, placing them in the middle of a square of cheesecloth or a tea towel, and then tying up the corners to create a bag. Place this in the bath and let it steep until the water is pleasantly scented.

Bath salts are another effective way of enjoying pleasant scents. Although you can make your own bath salts, I prefer to buy them, and choose fragrances that relate to my needs at the time. Ritual bathing is a good practice before any ritual, and the use of the correct bath salts enables you to become spiritually and intuitively in tune before the actual ritual commences. It may not always be necessary to bathe beforehand, but it helps you enter the right mental state to ensure a successful outcome. While relaxing in the bath, think of your goal and the desired outcome.

Soaps

Pleasant-smelling soaps can be a useful adjunct to any magical work. I buy good quality handmade soaps at a nearby craft store, but any soap that has the desired scent can be used. Soaps do much more than create a pleasant odor, of course, and it would be hard to think of anything better when engaged in purification work.

Pomanders

Pomanders were originally small china or metal containers that held spices and herbs. They were worn around the neck, or suspended from the girdle. Their aim was to protect the person from infections and unpleasant odors. Nowadays, traditional pomanders are seldom seen. However, you may occasionally see a folk pomander, which is a dried orange with cloves stuck into it. This produces a spicy fragrance that freshens the room and repels moths.

Pomanders of this sort are easy to make. All you need is a medium-sized, ripe orange and some whole cloves. Stick the cloves into the orange until it is completely covered, and then place it in a warm place to dry. In about two weeks the pomander will be ready for use.

You can tie a ribbon around the pomander, or perhaps wrap it in netting, and then hang it wherever you wish. The mixture of orange and cloves symbolize day and night, which means that a pomander of this sort will provide protection twenty-four hours a day.

Flowers

You should not forget the delicate perfume that flowers provide. Freshly cut flowers enhance the beauty of any environment. However, they should be discarded as soon as they start to die.

White flowers relate strongly to Gabriel. One especially magical example is Solomon's seal, a small flower with beautiful white, waxy blossoms. I like the white flowers that release their perfume at night. Night-scented stock, moon-daisies, and white narcissi are good examples.

White flowers can also bring you a month of good luck. All you need to do is place some white flowers in a crystal or cut-glass vase and put them in a window where the moon-light can caress them. They will absorb the moon's energies and grant you good fortune.

The lily has traditionally been considered the symbol of Gabriel, and many medieval paintings show Gabriel holding a lily. This is probably because white lilies are ruled by the Moon. Growing lilies, or having them in your home, is a good way to honor Gabriel and everything she does for you. Every time you happen to notice your lilies, smile and greet them as a gesture of love and respect.

Fragrances can be used on their own, or as part of a ritual. Smell is one of our strongest senses, and a scent can instantly bring back memories of previous occasions when we have smelled it. Incenses and other scents have been used throughout history to contact the angelic realms. Experiment with them yourself, and see how they will help you gain a closer connection with Gabriel.

Seven

GABRIEL AND WATER

WATER IS one of the basic necessities of life, and places where water appears have always been considered holy. Ancient people believed that any place where springs welled up out of the ground, rivers flowed, waterfalls cascaded, or lakes sat placidly, were all inhabited by divine spirits. They offered prayers and sacrifices to appease the water gods in the hope of receiving good fortune and to avert the possibility of disasters such as floods, or the drying up of sources of water.

The second verse of the Bible contains a remarkably evocative description: "The Spirit of God moved upon the face of the waters" (Genesis 1: 2). It is easy to imagine a face within moving water. It is also not difficult to picture God's face reflected on the surface of the waters.

The Elements

Ancient people believed that the world was created when the elements of fire, earth, air, and water came together to create order from chaos. These four elements are part of everything, and exist in the unseen, spiritual worlds, just as much as they do in the mundane, everyday world. In the unseen worlds, the four elements combine to form spirit, the life force in all living things. Because divine energy is made up of the four elements, we can use the elements to bring to us whatever it is we desire.

The first person known to have taught the concept of the four elements was Empedocles, a Sicilian who lived about 475 BCE. However, this concept is much older than Empedocles, and it plays a vital role in Assyrian, Egyptian, Greek, Hebrew, and Persian magical traditions. It was Aristotle (384–322 BCE) who introduced the four elements to the West, and over the last two thousand years they have played a major role in many traditions.

Over time, different associations were made with each of the elements. Some of the more common associations are listed below.

Fire

Plane: Spiritual

Astrological signs: Aries, Leo, Sagittarius

Metal: Gold

Direction: South

Color: Red (alternate color: orange)

Season: Summer

Jewel: Fire opal

Scent: Olibanum

Gender: Masculine

Angel: Michael

Earth

Plane: Physical

Astrological signs: Taurus, Virgo, Capricorn

Metal: Lead

Direction: North

Color: Green (alternate color: black)

Season: Winter

Jewel: Quartz

Scent: Storax

Gender: Feminine

Angel: Uriel

Air

Plane: Mental

Astrological signs: Gemini, Libra, Aquarius

Metal: Mercury

Direction: East

Color: Yellow (alternate colors: blue, white)

Season: Spring

Jewel: Topaz, chalcedony

Scent: Galbanum

Gender: Masculine

Angel: Raphael

Water

Plane: Emotional

Astrological signs: Cancer, Scorpio, Pisces

Metal: Silver

Direction: West

Color: Blue (alternate colors: silver, white)

Season: Autumn

Jewel: Aquamarine, beryl

Scent: Myrrh

Gender: Feminine

Angel: Gabriel

Many other associations can be made, ranging from evangelists to elementals, to gods and goddesses.

As you can see, Gabriel is associated with water. Consequently, we can use the water element to increase our closeness to Gabriel, and to gain messages and inspiration from her. Water can be found in many forms. If you live by an ocean, you are likely to take it for granted. However, someone who lives in, for instance, New Mexico, would probably be thrilled and excited at the prospect of spending time by the ocean. Obviously, there will be water wherever you live. It might be the sea, a lake, a river, stream, or even a creek. Any of these can be used to communicate with Gabriel.

Scrying

When people think of scrying they usually think of crystal ball gazing. However, scrying with water is much older. In the Bible, Joseph says: "Is not this it (the cup) in which my lord drinketh, and whereby indeed he divineth?" (Genesis 44:5). Cylicomancy, or divination with cups full of liquid, has always been one of the most commonly used methods of scrying in the East.[1]

No one knows where this form of divination began, but ancient historians such as Verro, Strabo, and Purchas felt that Persia was the most likely place. Divining cups are mentioned in both the *Rubaiyyat of Omar Khayyam* and *The Sháhnáma of Firdausi*, sometimes known as *The Book of Kings*. Abolgassem Firdausi (c. 935–1020 CE) was a poet and landowner who wrote his epic poem to provide a dowry for his daughter. Sadly, the Sultan gave him a pittance for the poem. Later on he relented, and sent sixty thousand dinars' worth of indigo to the poet, but it arrived too late. The poet was dead. In fact, the gift arrived at his funeral.

In his poem he wrote:

> *Then will I*
> *Call for the cup that mirroreth the world,*
> *And stand before God's presence. In that cup*
> *I shall behold the seven climes of earth,*

Both field and fell and all the provinces
Will offer reverence to mine ancestors,
My chosen, spacious lords, and then shalt know
Where thy son is. The cup will show me all.[2]

Damascius (480–550 CE), the last of the Platonic scholars at the Greek Academy at Athens, wrote of a holy woman
who scryed with a glass containing pure water.[3] Although
Damascius wrote that he had not personally witnessed this,
there are other contemporary accounts that give a clear picture of the process. Once the glass, or glasses, had been
filled with pure water, lighted torches were placed around
them. Once this was done, the question that had to be
divined was asked. Then, a young, innocent boy or a heavily pregnant woman was asked to carefully notice any
changes in the glasses, while at the same time demanding
an answer to the question from the glasses. The reflections
in the glasses usually provided the answer.[4]

There were also a number of oracle springs in Greece.
Pausanius mentioned three that were used for divination
purposes. The oracle of Apollo Thyrxeus revealed in the
water the answers to any questions. Unfortunately, the divination qualities were sometimes fragile. A renowned spring
at Taenarum lost its power when a woman washed her
dirty clothes in it.[5]

The earliest printed account of scrying in England dates
back to 1467. William Byg was charged with heresy, after
making his living as a scryer for two years. As punishment,
he had to walk at the head of a procession in York Cathedral with a lighted torch in his right hand, and his esoteric

books suspended from a stick in his left. He also had to recant and burn his books.[6]

There is a considerable amount of folklore concerning scrying. Until recently, girls in Lincolnshire visited the Maiden's Well to find out the identity of their future partner. They had to approach the well backwards, and then walk around the well three times in the same way. If they then looked into the spring, they would see the face of their future lover.[7] A similar practice has also been recorded on the island of Andros in Greece. Young girls would hold a mirror over a well to see their future husbands revealed in the reflection of the water.[8]

An extraordinary instance of spontaneous scrying was reported in the *Journal of the Society of Psychical Research* in December, 1903. A woman woke up during the night, picked up a glass of water from her bedside table, and before drinking from it, saw an image of a moving train in the water. As she watched, one carriage crashed into another. A couple of hours later, Mr. Leeds, her husband, arrived home and told her of an accident that had occurred at his work. It was exactly as she had seen it in her glass. The brakeman had been badly hurt.

Count Cagliostro (1743–1795) used young children when he scryed. As many of his experiments in this field were recorded by others, we know exactly how he worked. One such report was given at his trial for attempting to organize freemasonry in Italy in 1791. It said that a young child was placed on his knees in front of a table containing a large carafe of pure water. Behind the carafe were several lighted candles. Cagliostro performed an exorcism and then placed his hands on the boy's head. They both then prayed to God for the success of the experiment. The boy then looked into the carafe and told Cagliostro what he saw.

Count Beugnot, Minister of State to Napoleon I, wrote that Cagliostro was able to tell people what was happening in a distant city at the time the experiment was being performed in Paris. Alternatively, he could say what would be happening six days, six months, six years, or twenty years ahead. However, certain conditions were necessary before Cagliostro could do this. It was important that the child be pure and innocent. He or she also had to be born at a certain time, be highly intuitive, and have blue eyes. Usually a prepubescent child was an essential requirement, but Mademoiselle de Latour, a young woman, was one of Cagliostro's protégés. Apart from her age, she possessed all of the desired qualities. On at least one occasion, she saw the Archangel Gabriel inside the water. Gabriel obligingly gave her all the information that was required by Cardinal de Rohan who, with Cagliostro, was implicated in a complicated scandal known as the "Affair of the Diamond Necklace."[9]

Scrying with water has been practiced all around the world. One interesting variation was recorded by Sir Frank Swettenham, who met an Arab seer in Malaya. This man would fast and pray before pouring a small amount of water onto a small piece of paper that contained writing. The seer would see whatever he needed to know by gazing into the small pool of water.[10]

In Africa, scrying with water is common. The Zulus scry in the water held in their chief's vessel. Natives of the Kaonde and Alunda tribes can see both the past and the future in pools of river water.[11]

The purpose of scrying is to temporarily close off the critical, reasoning part of your mind, so that you become more receptive to the messages from your subconscious mind. This allows your intuition full flow. In this state, especially with water scrying, you become extremely receptive to any communications from Gabriel.

How to Scry with Water

Scrying is a skill that anyone can develop with practice. Some people take to it naturally, while others need to persevere until they get results. Experiment at different times of the day, and in different conditions. Some people prefer to scry in direct sunlight, while others need a partially darkened room. Some people like to have some sort of light, such as a candle, behind the glass of water they are scrying with. However, other scryers find this more of a hindrance than a help. Again, some people like to place their glass on a dark surface, such as black velvet, while for others it makes no difference what surface the glass rests on. As everyone is different, you will have to experiment until you find the right combination for you.

You will need a plain glass. You do not want one that contains ridges or designs on the outside. The plainer the glass, the better. Fill this glass about three-quarters full with water, and then set it down on a suitable surface.

Sit so that you can gaze downward into the glass. The surface of the water should be a comfortable reading distance from your eyes. However, don't gaze at the surface of the water. Instead, look through the surface into the water below.

There is no need to eliminate thoughts, or to strain, or even to concentrate. Simply gaze into the water and see what happens. If you are fortunate, you will see results almost immediately. If you have not scryed before, you may not see anything the first few times you experiment.

There is no ideal length of time to practice. Gaze into the water until your eyes feel tired. There is no point in carrying on after you reach this state. Put the glass away and practice again later.

Sometimes you will find yourself directly inside a vision. At other times the water may appear to cloud or darken first, before the visions start. An acquaintance of mine says the water always goes milky before the visions commence. However, I have also spoken to people who experienced different sensations. One of my students said the surface of the water became dappled for several seconds before the visions appeared. Many of my students see what appear to be gently floating, fluffy clouds. Others have said they experience a sudden feeling of peace, which tells them that the visions are about to start. You may experience one or more of these, or you may experience something completely different.

The results you see will vary. Usually, the glass and its surroundings will seem to temporarily disappear, and you will find yourself watching a vision of some sort. If you are scrying for a specific purpose, what you see will be related to that, although that may not seem to be the case until you think about it later. If you are scrying out of simple curiosity, the visions could be about almost anything, although they are likely to be related to what is going on in your life at the time of the experiment. If you are scrying to make contact with Gabriel, you may see Gabriel in the glass, but are more likely to see visions that relate to your reasons for contacting her. Do not be disappointed if you do not see Gabriel. That may occur later. Take heed of the visions you see, and then act on them.

You may be scrying to gain insights into your future. This can be a helpful exercise, especially if you have two or more possible directions in which you can go. You can look at each possibility in turn to see which scenario appeals to you most. You can then ask Gabriel for her advice as to which one you should pursue.

You are in a state while scrying that is similar to daydreaming. If something happened to disturb you, you would instantly be returned to your everyday world. Many years ago, one of my students was concerned that she could be subject to outside attack while scrying, because she felt that she was in an altered state. However, this is not possible. Scrying is perfectly safe.

Scrying and Automatic Writing

Automatic writing is an interesting phenomenon that occurs when your hand, holding a pen, writes messages while you are relaxing or doing something else. Over the years, many books have been written this way. It seems as if someone or something else takes control of your writing hand, and creates messages that can be surprising and unexpected.

You can practice automatic writing whenever you have some free time. If you are relaxing in front of the television, for instance, try holding a pen on a pad of paper, and see what happens. The important part is to simply let it happen. Do not react when you feel your hand starting to move. Wait until you're finished, and then check to see what you have produced. When you start, you are likely to produce scribbles or circles and ellipses. However, words will gradually start to come, and you'll be amazed at just how quickly your hand can write words with no conscious input from you.

Using a combination of scrying and automatic writing is a highly effective way to receive messages from Gabriel. Sit in front of the glass you are using for scrying. Place a pad of writing paper on the table beside the glass, and rest your writing hand on it, holding a pencil or pen. It is important that the table is sturdy, as you do not want the motions of your writing hand to create movement in the water.

Scry in the normal way, but ask Gabriel to bring you a message. The message will come in one of three ways. You may see the answer inside the glass, you may receive a written message obtained by automatic writing, or you may receive both.

Water Gazing in Everyday Life

You can water-gaze wherever you find water. With practice, you will find that you can water-gaze effectively by gazing into the running water of a brook, stream, or river. You can also do it by gazing into the waters of a lake or ocean. I find it best to focus on the shimmering of the sun on the water's surface while doing this.

Sit down in a comfortable spot where you can gaze at the water. Allow yourself to relax, and watch the gentle movement of the water, or the shimmering of the sun on the surface. Think about your purpose in water-gazing and see what comes into your mind. If you find yourself thinking random thoughts about something completely different, gently bring your mind back to your purpose. In time, something that relates to your purpose will appear in your mind. Ask questions about the matter, and see what other information comes to you.

You can also water-gaze in this way when you do not have a specific question. This turns it into a kind of meditation, and random thoughts will come to you. Pursue the thoughts that appear interesting, and gently discard the others.

It is unusual to see visions in large bodies of water, but it does occur. If you are fortunate, you will see pictures appearing in the water whenever you scry in this way, but for most people it is a rare occurrence.

Wave Scrying

Obviously, this method can only be used if you live close to the sea. If you have ever stood for any length of time watching the movements of the waves, you will know just how hypnotic they can be. The best time to scry with the waves is at night, with the moonlight dancing on the crests of the waves.

Sit down somewhere where you can gaze at the waves, and allow their movement to take you into a slightly altered state. This is the same feeling that you experience on a cold winter's evening when you sit by the fire and gaze into the flames. You tend to blink less, and gradually feel yourself being pulled into whatever it is you are gazing at. This is why you should always sit down before performing this exercise.

Once you have reached this state, ask for an answer to your concerns, or simply wait and see what comes to you. You will be amazed at what comes into your mind. The insights and information that you receive this way could not be achieved with any other method.

There is one caveat with sea scrying, however. Because the hypnotic effects of the waves are so powerful, you should only do it if you are certain that you will not be drawn into the sea. Extremely suggestible people should restrict their water-scrying to small containers of water in their homes.

The Sounds of Scrying

As a child, I am sure you dipped a finger into a glass of liquid and then made a sound by drawing your wet finger around the rim of the glass. This was used as a method of scrying more than a thousand years ago. Michael Constantius Psellus (1020–1105 CE) may have been referring to this when he wrote in his book, *De daemonibus:*

> *When the water begins to lend itself as the vehicle of sound, the spirit also presently gives out a thin reedy note of satisfaction, but devoid of meaning; and close upon that, whilst the water is undulating, certain weak and peeping sounds whisper forth predictions of the future.*[12]

In his book, *Scrying for Beginners*, Donald Tyson suggests that Nostradamus may have produced his predictions by drawing a wand around the rim of the vessel, and using his guardian angel to interpret the sounds. He probably also saw visions in the basin.[13]

If you would like to try this method, find a large, deep bowl. Place this on a tripod, or short base, to allow it to resonate clearly. You will need to experiment to find the right level of water. Start by filling the bowl three-quarters full, and then slowly add more water until it works well.

You will need a wand to draw around the rim of the container. Traditionally, a branch of the laurel tree was used. However, apple, bay, hazel, pear, and willow also work well. Your wand should be between six and eighteen inches in length. Again, experimentation is required to find the length that works best for you. If you are unable to procure a suitable wand, you can use the forefinger of your dominant hand. However, this should only be used as a temporary measure.

Dip the end of the wand into the water until it is thoroughly wet, and then slowly draw it around the rim of the bowl. You may have to experiment to find the right level of wetness, amount of pressure required, and correct angle of the wand against the bowl's rim.

Once you can produce a continuous tone, gaze into the center of the bowl while continuing to run the wand around the rim of the bowl. This movement will create ripples in the bowl. Listen intently for the soft, faint tones that lie under the heavier, dominant sound. Nostradamus thought that this sound was a message from heaven. I believe it is more likely to be Archangel Gabriel talking to you. Once you can sense this soft, gentle, feminine tone, stop the movements of your wand, and listen to the fainter tones while gazing into the water. You may hear whispered words, see images in the bowl, or receive impressions in your mind. Follow whatever comes for as long as you can. You can stop at this point if you have received a detailed answer. If you need more information, go through the process as many times as necessary to learn what you need to know.

Wishing Wells

Tossing a coin into a well is an extremely old practice. The ancient Greeks did it to appease the water gods, thinking that if they tossed coins into a well it wouldn't run dry. Appeasing the water gods has always been done in the belief that it brings good luck.

There is a tradition that if you toss a coin into a well or fountain, and then wait for the water to become still enough to see your reflection in it, any wish you then make will be granted by the water gods. A variation of this can be seen today when honeymooners at Niagara Falls toss coins into the Bridal Veil Falls to ensure good fortune and a happy marriage.

Wishing wells were also used as scrying bowls. A girl who wanted to marry would toss a coin into a well, in the hope that she would see her future husband's face in the water in the well. This was normally done at full moon, because the moon has always been considered beneficial to matters concerning love and romance.

Wishing wells and springs are excellent places to contact Gabriel. Find a suitable offering such as a smooth pebble or small coin and toss it into the well or spring. Give thanks for all the blessings in your life, and then ask Gabriel to join you. Sit down comfortably, close to the well or spring, and enjoy communing with nature and conversing with Gabriel. This is not usually a time to ask Gabriel for her help. It is better to use this form of contact to thank Gabriel for her help in every part of your life.

Pond Magic

When I was very young, we lived close to a small creek. I used to play there with other local children. One of the things we did was to ask a question that could be answered with a simple "yes" or "no." We would then toss a small pebble into the creek and count the number of rings that the stone created. An odd answer meant "yes," while an even answer indicated "no."

We boys were more interested in catching water boatmen, small insects that flitted over the surface of the water, but the girls seemed to have more respect for the sacredness of the spot. One of the older girls always brought a saucer of milk that she left for the water gods. Although, at the time I had no idea why she was doing this, I accepted that she knew what she was doing. The fact that the milk always disappeared convinced us all of the reality of water gods.

Small pools of water such as ponds and creeks make effective scrying instruments. I particularly like doing this near the full moon. Sit or lie down and gaze at the moon's reflection in the surface of the water. Relax and see what thoughts or visions come to you.

Water Meditation

Gabriel can help you any time you feel out of your depth, or are scared about taking the plunge. You can do this exercise anywhere, at any time. I like to do it beside a body of water, if possible, but that is not necessary. You might prefer to do this exercise in bed before going to sleep.

Lie down comfortably and consciously relax your body as much as possible. Visualize yourself lying beside a beautiful lake. You might choose a lakeside scene that you are familiar with, or you might use your imagination to create a pleasant scene. I picture a lake, high up in the mountains, that I visited frequently when I was a child. Visualize the surroundings, and enjoy the gentle sounds of the lapping water.

In your imagination, ask Gabriel to join you. Because you are imagining this scene, you might like to picture her walking across the lake to be with you. She might descend from the clouds, or appear from nowhere.

Visualize yourself smiling at each other, and then see yourself get up and walk hand-in-hand with Gabriel around the lake. You might feel the dewy grass beneath your feet, and you will surely smell the crisp, fresh country air.

For a while, you and Gabriel talk about inconsequential matters, and then she will ask you what is on your mind. See yourself replying, explaining whatever it is that is concerning you. Notice how much better you feel once you have told Gabriel the full story.

Gabriel smiles at you, and then begins to give you valuable advice. You nod your head in agreement now and again. Once Gabriel has finished you might have a few more questions, which Gabriel cheerfully answers. You notice that the two of you have stopped walking and are standing on a small beach beside the lake. Gabriel picks up a smooth pebble and sends it skimming out onto the lake.

It bounces several times before disappearing. You laugh, and pick up a pebble yourself. For several minutes you and Gabriel forget your problems, and contentedly skim pebbles on the lake.

You both stop skimming pebbles at the same time. You gaze into Gabriel's eyes and thank her for all her advice and support. She asks you if you understood everything she told you. You tell her that you have, and that you will act on it. Gabriel squeezes your hand, and then disappears.

You sit down close to the water's edge and think about the advice Gabriel has given you. When you feel ready, you open your eyes and stretch.

Some of my students felt that this entire exercise was imaginary. I asked them about the advice they received from Gabriel. "Was it good advice?" I asked. "Was it relevant to what is going on in your life?" They all replied "yes." "In that case," I continued, "Does it matter if the exercise is real or imaginary?"

It is possible that you may feel the same way that my students did. As long as the advice you receive is good, it obviously makes no difference how real the experience was. However, after performing it a few times, I am sure that you will, like my students, come to believe that it is a real encounter with Gabriel, and perform it often.

Cup Magic

You can use any teacup for magical purposes, but it is a good idea to have a special cup that you keep for magical use.

Fill a large bowl with water, and then plunge your teacup into it. The cup is now obviously full of water. Keeping the cup in the bowl, turn it upside down. Although it is still full of water, you have symbolically emptied it. Lift it out of the bowl while it is still upside down. This naturally empties it of water, but fills it with air. Turn it over and breathe air into the cup. As you do this, think loving thoughts about your special cup. This charges the cup with your essence.

Once you have done this, you can use the cup for a variety of purposes. If you need more enthusiasm, vitality, and energy, fill the cup with direct sunlight and then "drink" it. If you want love in your life, or want to be more intuitive, fill the cup with light from the moon, and drink it.

If you want to change your life in any way, use the cup as an aid. Breathe into it any bad habits, or anything else that you want to eliminate from your life, and turn the cup upside down over a rubbish bin or garbage disposal. Once you have done this, turn the cup right-side-up again and breathe love and thanks into it.

You can also use the cup to make a special blessing to Gabriel. Start by filling the cup with water. Hold it in your cupped hands while thanking Gabriel for all the blessings she has brought into your life. Fill the cup with love. Then pour the water over or around some live plants. I normally water my potted plants this way. This blessed and sacred water will do wonders for your plants, as they naturally respond to your thoughts, which have been transfused into the water.

Once you have used the cup for some time, you will be able to use it to see Gabriel. Fill the cup with water. Gaze into the water until you feel you are totally relaxed. Think of someone who had a major, positive influence on your life. Ideally, this will be someone you have not thought of for many years. In my case, I think of Miss Smallfield, my teacher when I was eight years old. Continue gazing into the water until you see a clear picture of that person's face in the bowl. Once you can see that person clearly in the water, say "thank you" out loud. This is to thank that particular person for everything they did for you. Next you have to think of someone you loved deeply. This could be a first love, or possibly a parent or other relative. Again, it should be someone you have not thought about for a long time. Wait until you see that person's face in the water. Again give thanks. This is important. Even if the relationship ended badly, the love must have been there at one time, as otherwise you would not have chosen this person. Finally, think of Gabriel. Wait patiently until you can see Gabriel's face in the water. Once you see her, say whatever you wish to say. At the end of the communication, thank her and kiss the cup. This water will be thrice blessed, and will help any plant you offer it to.

Whenever you finish working with your cup, fill it with love and kiss it before putting it away until the next time you use it.

Gabriel Water

It is also possible to drink water that has been blessed by Gabriel. You will find that it tastes subtly different from ordinary drinking water.

All you need to do is fill a glass with ordinary water and let it stand in the direct rays of the moon for at least one hour. After this time, hold the glass with both hands at shoulder height, facing the moon. Thank Gabriel for all her efforts on your behalf, and then drink the water. You will find the water cool, refreshing, energizing, and health giving. It will also send Gabriel's energies to every cell of your body.

Gabriel water can also be used at the time of the full moon by couples desiring a baby. It is best to perform this ritual outdoors if possible. You can also perform it indoors, just as long as you can see the full moon from where you are working. Light a silver candle and allow it to be bathed by the rays of the moon. Pour a glass or goblet of drinking water, and place it in front of the candle. Look at the moon, summon Gabriel, and tell her how much you would love to have a baby. Picture yourself nursing a sleeping baby, and allow your feelings of love and tenderness to enfold you. Thank Gabriel for her love, and tell her again of your desire to have a child. When you feel ready, put out the candle in the glass of water, and then drink the water in a single draught. This ritual needs to be performed for nine full moons in succession. The same candle is used each time, and the stub is allowed to burn away to nothing on the night of the last full moon. The ritual needs to be performed in exactly the same way each time. It is important not to allow feelings of hopelessness or desperation to creep into your thoughts. Remain positive and allow Gabriel to work for your best interests. Obviously, if you become pregnant during this nine-month period, you can stop performing the ritual.

Some people like to place a crystal in the glass of water before energizing it in the moon's glow. Moonstone is ideal for this, but any crystal that symbolizes Gabriel will work well. We will be looking at suitable crystals and gemstones in the next chapter.

Eight

GABRIEL AND CRYSTALS

CRYSTALS and gemstones have always been considered precious objects. Ancient people marveled at the beauty of these stones and believed that they were the source of Mother Earth's healing, nurturing power. Gemstones have been found in prehistoric burial grounds in many parts of the world.

Many people believe that people started wearing gemstones as protective amulets, rather than as items of adornment. Regardless of the original motivations, crystals and gemstones are just as sought after today as they ever were.

It is natural that certain stones were used as amulets. Apart from their brilliance and color, the forms they appeared in had an immediate effect on ancient people. Staurolite, for instance, contains twined crystals that form the shape of a cross. In many cases, specimens of staurolite are so perfect that you would swear that a skilled craftsman had carved them. They are frequently sold as "fairy stone" or "twin stone."

Color played an important role, also. It is not surprising that red stones reminded people of blood, or that blue stones had a connection with both water and the sky. In time, red stones came to be used to stop bleeding.

The energy that certain stones contain was noticed early on. The ancient Romans were fascinated with the magnetic powers of the lodestone, and speculated that other stones also emitted power and energy. Alexander the Great gave lodestone to his soldiers, as he believed it would protect his men from pain, as well as evil spirits.[1]

Theophrastus (c. 372–287 BCE) wrote the first book specifically on gemstones. Unfortunately, only a fragment of this work, entitled *Peri Lithon* (*On Stones*) survives. Pliny the Elder (23–79 CE) wrote a thirty-seven volume work called *Historia Naturalis*, which contained a large amount of information on crystals and gems. Since its first publication in 77 CE it has appeared in more than 250 editions, in many different languages. Pliny is credited with being the first person to classify gems by color and other characteristics.

Crystals have always been considered an effective way of gaining contact with the angelic realm. Any blue or white crystal that you find attractive and appealing will work well for you. Traditionally, lapis lazuli has been used to gain a close connection with Gabriel. However, many people use lapis lazuli to contact Michael. This shows that you can use any gemstone you personally like to contact the archangels. Clear quartz can also be used to contact any member of the angelic realms.

Gemstones can be used in various ways to help you gain contact with Gabriel. Wearing them or carrying them with you as an amulet ensures that Gabriel is close to you at all times. You can even sleep with your stone under your pillow. When necessary, you can easily touch the stone to gain instant contact.

Lapis Lazuli

Lapis lazuli is composed of lazurite, pyrite, and calcite. The lazurite provides the deep blue color, while the pyrite adds the beautiful gold flecks. Because of its beauty, it is not surprising that it was worth just as much as gold in ancient times. Lapis lazuli was considered the ultimate stone to be worn by royalty. One description of Innini, a Babylonian goddess, said that she wore lapis lazuli brooches and other adornments, including a necklace containing large stones of lapis lazuli.[2] The Sumerians believed that anyone who carried lapis lazuli as an amulet was actually carrying a god with them.[3] The ancient Egyptians made amulets of lapis lazuli in the form of an eye. It was inscribed with the 140th chapter of the *Book of the Dead*, and was considered an amulet of enormous power.[4] The chief justice also wore around his neck an image of Ma'at (the Goddess of Truth) made from lapis lazuli.

In the Middle Ages, lapis lazuli was considered a cure for depression. Chevalier John de Mandeville wrote that it prevented conception if worn by either the man or woman. It was also powdered and turned into an expensive, but highly desired paint: ultramarine.

Along with sapphire and other blue stones, lapis lazuli was believed to offset the negative forces of the spirits of darkness, and to aid the assistance of the spirits of light.

You can use lapis lazuli to help you develop your intuition, promote clear thinking, encourage purification, and remember your dreams. Wearing or carrying lapis lazuli with you will allow this to occur. This also enables you to touch the lapis lazuli whenever you need instant help or protection from Gabriel. You can use lapis lazuli to enhance any rituals involving Gabriel.

Aquamarine

Until 1609, aquamarine was known as blue-green beryl. It was first referred to as aquamarine in *Gemmarum et Lapidum Historia* by Anselmus de Boodt.[5] Aquamarine has always been considered the stone of clarity. If you are in need of Gabriel's help in this area, aquamarine is the perfect stone to wear or carry.

Blue Topaz

Topaz was used in ancient times to ward off the evil eye. It was sometimes tied to the left arm, where it protected its owners from curses. In the thirteenth century, The Hindu physician Naharare recommended topaz as a remedy for flatulence. He also claimed that any man who wore it would be intelligent, good looking, and enjoy a long life.[6]

Blue topaz provides guidance and inspiration. It helps you to change unwanted thinking patterns, and to become emotionally freer.

Blue Tourmaline

Blue tourmaline is rare, and you will have to search hard to find it. Traditionally, it eliminates negativity and helps achievement of goals.

Chalcedony

Chalcedony varies in color, being found in white, gray, and blue. White and blue are the correct forms to use if the stone is going to be dedicated to Gabriel. Chalcedony is commonly referred to as the orator's stone, as it is believed to aid the voice and provide confidence when you have to think and speak on your feet. Traditionally, chalcedony provides serenity, peace of mind, and generosity. It is a good stone to carry if you are seeking purification from a past negative experience.

Lavender Quartz

Lavender quartz is white in color, and is not easy to find. It is usually more expensive than other quartzes. It enhances intuition, vision, and inspiration. It also provides energy and eliminates doubts and fears.

Milky Quartz

This is a milky-white stone that comes from Brazil. It provides peace, harmony, and compassion. It also helps provide love and forgiveness.

Moonstone

The moonstone appeals to many people because of its close relationship with the psychic and spiritual realms. It makes a good choice if you are contacting Gabriel for help in developing your psychic abilities, or are seeking visions of angelic guidance. Moonstone is available in a variety of shades. White moonstone is the best choice when working with Gabriel.

Pearl

The pearl has been prized throughout history, and is considered to symbolize faith, charity, serenity, purity, innocence, and goodness. Pliny the Elder wrote that pearls were formed from "dews of heaven" that fell into the sea and were caught by oysters. The quality of the pearl varied, depending on the quality of the dew and the weather conditions at the time it fell into the sea. Pure dew naturally created perfect pearls. However, cloudy conditions caused the pearls to be discolored and dull. Thunder caused the oysters to miscarry and lose the pearl.[7]

Pearls were considered so valuable in Egyptian times that Cleopatra drank a toast to Mark Anthony that contained a dissolved pearl. The pearl was said to have been more valuable than the rest of the feast combined, and was intended to make Mark Anthony understand the incredible wealth of Egypt.

Because of their association with purity, pearls are the ideal stone if you need purification. As a bonus, they are traditionally believed to warn you of impending disaster.

Sapphire

It is believed that the ten commandments were inscribed on large tablets of sapphire. Certainly, sapphire has been considered a sacred gem for thousands of years. In the second century BCE, Damigeron, the Greek historian, wrote that kings wear sapphire around their necks for protection. He continued to say that sapphire prevented envy, and made people agreeable to God.[8] The Roman Catholic Church believes that the sapphire promotes chastity and banishes evil thoughts. Consequently, bishops wear rings of sapphire.

Sapphire is a good stone to use if you need purification or time to think. It is believed to be restorative to the mind, body, and soul, enabling the wearer to achieve inner peace. Not surprisingly, it is sometimes referred to as the philosopher's stone.

Selenite

Selenite is considered one of the most powerful healing stones. It works well with Gabriel, and can be used to help eliminate feelings of guilt, and to let go of the past. Selenite also calms the emotions, and helps to clarify thoughts.

Tanzanite

Tanzanite was unknown until 1967, when it was discovered in northern Tanzania.[9] It quickly became popular because of its deep blue color, the fact that it was cheaper than sapphire, and because it changes color as you move it. These colors range from blue to purple to pink. Tanzanite is a good crystal to carry if you are seeking guidance from Gabriel. Tanzanite also balances the mind, body, and spirit.

Turquoise

Turquoise was valued and prized by the Babylonians, Egyptians, Aztecs, Mayas, and Incas. The Persians considered it their national stone, and even had a saying about it: "To avoid evil and attain good fortune one must see the reflection of the new moon either on the face of a friend, on a copy of the Koran, or on a turquoise."[10]

Cleansing Your Crystal

Any crystals that are dedicated to Gabriel will need to be cleansed occasionally. It is important that they be thoroughly cleansed as soon as possible after buying them. A good way to do this is to place them in a container of salt water overnight. The salt breaks down the energy stored inside the crystal, and the water cleanses and absorbs the crystal's energies.

Crystals dedicated to Gabriel will not need to be cleansed very often. They can be cleansed by passing them through a candle flame, by placing them in salt water overnight, or by burying them in the ground for twenty-four hours. You can also cleanse them with prayers. If you are in a hurry, simply hold the crystal under running water for a minute or two.

It is a simple matter to energize your crystal. Sit down comfortably, with the stone of your choice between the thumb and index finger of your minor hand. This is your left hand if you are right-handed, and your right if you are left-handed. Breathe on the crystal to remove any negative energies. Turn the crystal around to ensure that you breathe on every part. Rest the back of the hand holding the crystal on the palm of the other hand, and raise your hands until they are about chest height.

Close your eyes and ask Gabriel to join you. When you feel her presence, ask her to energize the crystal. You are likely to feel a tingling sensation in the palm of your hand as the crystal becomes energized. Some people feel a sudden coolness in the hand. Once the crystal has become fully energized, close your fingers over the crystal, and thank Gabriel for doing this for you. Discuss anything you wish with Gabriel, and then thank her again as you say goodbye. The crystal is now energized and filled with Gabriel's healing energy.

You can wash your crystals at any time by holding them under running water for about five minutes. This does not affect the energizing power provided by Gabriel.

If you want to energize your crystal with masculine energy, charge the crystal with sunlight. Likewise, if you want feminine energy, bathe it in moonlight.

Remember that your crystals absorb your thoughts and feelings. Be as positive and upbeat as possible while in their presence. Cleanse the crystals any time you feel they have been exposed to negative energy.

Crystal Meditation

Once you have found the right crystal, you will be able to use it in many ways. You may decide that you want a number of crystals, for different purposes. There is no need to restrict yourself. I regularly buy crystals that appeal to me. However, you should keep the crystals that are dedicated to Gabriel separate from other crystals you may have. After cleansing and charging them, I either display them somewhere where they can radiate light and energy, or as an alternative, wrap them in silk and put them away. Obviously, the displayed crystals need to be dusted regularly. I also never allow anyone else to handle my Gabriel crystals. I have plenty of crystals that I let other people hold, but I prefer not to allow anyone else's vibrations to affect the crystals I have dedicated to Gabriel.

Your crystal will respond to regular use. Once you have chosen the right crystal for you, carry it around with you, hold it, stroke it, and handle it as often as possible. Every now and then, while doing this, you will gain sudden insight into matters that are going on in your life. This will be a message from Gabriel.

A crystal meditation with Gabriel is highly restorative, and you will want to perform it regularly. There are nine steps to the meditation.

1. Choose a time and place when you will not be disturbed. A sacred place near your altar would be perfect, but anywhere where you can temporarily cut yourself off from the outside world will work well.

2. Sit down quietly, with your crystal in your left hand. Close your eyes and ask Gabriel for help, guidance, and protection.

3. Relax yourself as much as possible. You can do this is a variety of ways. You may consciously relax all the muscles in your body, starting with your feet and working your way up through the body. You might prefer to tense and then relax different muscle groups until you are completely relaxed. If you do this, start by squeezing your eyes tightly shut, and then relaxing the muscles around your eyes. Most of the time, I find this is all I need to do. Once those muscles are relaxed, everything else seems to relax automatically.

4. Imagine yourself totally surrounded in a circle of white light that provides protection, and even more relaxing energy. I visualize this white light descending from the heavens and enfolding me in its healing, protective light.

5. Mentally focus on the crystal in your left hand. Visualize a stream of blue light connecting the crystal and your third eye (the area just above your eyes, between your eyebrows).

6. Ask Gabriel to join you. When you feel her presence, ask her to charge the crystal with divine energy. Let her hold the crystal, if she wishes. Discuss any problems or difficulties you may have with her. Listen closely for the answers, which are likely to come as thoughts in your mind.

7. When you feel ready, thank Gabriel for constantly looking after you, and for the difference she is making in your life. Hold the crystal up high, and say goodbye.

8. Once Gabriel has gone, sit quietly for a few minutes. Different thoughts will appear in your mind. Think about them. When you are ready, take three slow, deep breaths and open your eyes.

9. Take a minute or two to evaluate what has happened before carrying on with your day. It is a good idea to write down everything you remember while the experience is still fresh in your mind. Different thoughts that seem insignificant at the time might have much more relevance later. Record as much as possible.

How Your Gabriel Crystal Can Enable You to Achieve Your Desires

Naturally, Gabriel wants you to lead a happy, fulfilling life. You are not likely to be happy if you are constantly desiring things that are out of reach. Fortunately, Gabriel, through your crystal, can help you achieve these goals.

Hold your crystal for a few minutes while you clarify in your mind exactly what it is you wish to achieve. Once it is clear in your mind, hold your crystal against your third eye, the area between your eyebrows. This is where your sixth chakra is found. We will be discussing that in the next chapter.

Think about your desire. Close your eyes and visualize it as clearly as possible. In your mind's eye, see yourself as if you have already attained the goal. If you want to buy a new car, for instance, picture yourself walking into the car dealership and taking the car for a test drive. See yourself coming back and paying for the car. Finally, see yourself driving home in it. Feel it in as many ways as possible. You might enjoy the smell of a brand new car. You can sense how smoothly it drives. A friend of mine bought a new car recently. When I asked him why he had bought that particular car, he said, "Because it makes me feel good." Allow yourself to feel good as you drive home in your new car.

Finally, thank Gabriel for making it possible for you to achieve your goals. Allow yourself to briefly experience all of these feelings every time you handle that particular stone. Repeat this exercise regularly until you achieve your goal. Remember to thank Gabriel each time you do the exercise, and especially when your goal has been realized.

Using Your Crystal for Purification

The energies stored inside your crystal can help you purify yourself, release any negativity from the past, and achieve peace of mind. One remarkable fact about a crystal that is dedicated to Gabriel is that most of these things will start happening automatically if you keep your crystal on you at all times. Different matters will come up to the surface of your mind, but will no longer have the power they used to have. You will be able to look at them calmly and dismiss them, as you no longer want them in your life.

There is also a simple exercise you can do that will speed up the process. Although this exercise can sometimes be done in as little as ten minutes, it is best to set aside at least one hour, as it is impossible to determine what matters will surface while you are doing it.

Lie down somewhere where you will not be disturbed, and place your crystal over the area of your heart. The terminated (pointed) end should be facing your chin. Relax and think pleasant thoughts. After a minute or two, you will suddenly find a variety of unresolved hurts and traumas will come to the surface. You are likely to feel highly emotional, and you should give these emotions free rein. Cry, yell, kick the floor, and do whatever else is necessary to eliminate these emotions. You will find that they will disappear as quickly and as suddenly as they began.

Do not get up too quickly after this has occurred. Allow yourself to release all the hurts and grievances that have surfaced. You might like to speak out loud, saying something along the lines of: "I now release all the negativity that was stored inside me. I am now purified in mind, body and spirit. Thank you, Gabriel, for cleansing my mind, body, and spirit from (whatever it happens to be). I love myself. I accept myself unconditionally. I am a perfect human being."

Think about what has happened, and thank Gabriel for allowing you to become purified and whole again. When you feel ready, get up and carry on with your day. You are likely to feel lighter, freer, and a great deal happier than you were before performing the exercise. Hold the crystal in your cupped hands, thank it, and allow your hands, and your entire body, to become filled with Gabriel's energy.

Some of my students had no success when they first performed this exercise. I was surprised to learn this, as some of them needed purification after sexual assault and burglary. Once I thought about it, the answer was obvious. These people were subconsciously holding on to the hurt and pain. If this situation applies to you, perform this exercise regularly until you achieve release. Your crystal, filled with Gabriel's love and energy, ensures that purification will occur, even though it might take longer than you consciously wish.

Two of the exercises in this chapter involved the chakras. We will see how Gabriel can help you with your chakras in the next chapter.

Nine

GABRIEL AND THE CHAKRAS

THE HUMAN body is a complex network of energy. Inside the aura and located along the spinal column are seven energy centers, or batteries, known as chakras. They play a vital role in the correct functioning of every part of the body, and are influenced by thoughts and feelings. When they are balanced, and operating efficiently, life runs smoothly, and we enjoy happiness, contentment, and good health. When one or more of the chakras is out of balance, or becomes blocked, the body ceases to work efficiently, and we experience dis-ease, mentally and/or physically.

Although the chakras cannot be proven to exist physically, they can be seen by clairvoyants as whirling circles of energy. In fact, the word "chakra" comes from the Sanskrit word for "wheel." Although most people cannot see them, it is a simple matter to demonstrate their existence. If, for example, you are unable to express something, you will experience a lump in your throat. The throat chakra is located here and is concerned with communication. When you experience a moment of pure love, you will feel it in the area of your heart. Not surprisingly, the heart chakra is concerned with love. The keywords for each chakra are given below. Experiment by saying them to yourself, and see if you can feel your body's response.

Here are the seven chakras:

Root Chakra

Color: Red

Keywords: I have

Archangel: Sandalphon

Element: Earth

The root chakra is sometimes called the base chakra. It is situated at the base of the spine, and keeps us grounded. The root chakra is concerned with security and survival. Once our survival needs are taken care of, we can focus on other aspects of our lives.

Sacral Chakra

Color: Orange

Keywords: I want, I feel, I desire

Archangels: Gabriel, Chamuel

Element: Water

The sacral chakra is situated between the navel and the genitals. It is concerned with sexuality, the emotions, pleasure, and creativity. When it is blocked, the person is likely to be lustful, angry, greedy, and overly emotional. Because this chakra is related to the water element, some people with blocked sacral chakras weep easily.

Solar Plexus Chakra

Color: Yellow

Keywords: I can, I will

Archangels: Uriel, Michael, Jophiel

Element: Fire

The solar plexus chakra is situated slightly above the navel. It is concerned with confidence, courage, power, and physical energy. When we get nervous, we lack power or control, and get butterflies in the stomach.

Heart Chakra

Color: Green and Pink

Keywords: I love

Archangels: Raphael, Chamuel

Element: Air

The heart chakra is located in the center of the chest in the area of the heart. It is concerned with healing, love, and compassion. It is common for this chakra to be blocked. If someone experiences a loss and fails to go through the grieving process, they will cause damage to this chakra. All emotional trauma causes blockages in this chakra.

Throat Chakra

> *Color:* Blue
>
> *Keywords:* I speak
>
> *Archangel:* Michael
>
> *Element:* Sound

The throat chakra is located in the center of the throat. It is concerned with creativity and communication, especially verbal communication. We become shy and uncommunicative when this chakra is blocked. Conversely, we talk far too much, and forget to listen, when this chakra is wide open.

Brow Chakra

> *Color:* Indigo
>
> *Keywords:* I see
>
> *Archangels:* Gabriel, Jophiel
>
> *Element:* Light

The brow chakra is situated between the eyebrows. It is sometimes known as the third eye chakra, and is concerned with psychic and intuitive perception. It is also related to wisdom, memory, higher consciousness, dreams, and vision.

Crown Chakra

  Color: Violet

  Keywords: I know

  Archangel: Zadkiel

  Element: Thought

The crown chakra is situated at the top of the head. It is our connection with the divine. It is concerned with consciousness, understanding, acceptance, and awareness. Information comes into this chakra and is distributed through all the others to achieve results.

Many people subconsciously focus on one or two chakras at the expense of the others. Someone who is focused on the second and third chakras (sexuality and physical energy) will be concerned primarily with power, domination, and sexual conquest. He or she will have a desperate desire to win all the time.

Someone who is focused on the root chakra will be concerned solely with survival. He or she will be concerned only with food, shelter, and other basic needs. Someone who focused on the sacral chakra will be concerned with sensual gratification, and will seek food, sex, possessions, and wealth. He or she will be largely concerned with satisfying emotional needs. Someone who is focused on the solar plexus chakra will be aggressive and emotional. He or she will have little interest or concern with spiritual or other higher concerns.

The qualities become more attractive with people who are focused on one of the higher chakras. Someone who is focused on the heart chakra will both accept and give unconditional love to everyone. Someone who is focused on the throat chakra will be highly expressive and will speak his or her truth. Someone who is focused on the brow chakra will be a highly intuitive clairvoyant or visionary. He or she will be wise and possess significant insight. Someone who is focused on the crown chakra will be highly spiritual.

You can probably think of many people who are focusing on the lower chakras, especially the bottom two, but it might be hard to think of anyone who is solely concerned with one of the higher chakras. For a good and healthy life, we naturally want the same amount of attention to be paid to every chakra.

Chakra Balancing

There are many ways to balance the chakras. One simple method involves using a pendulum. A pendulum is a small weight attached to a thread or chain. Any small weight will do. My mother used to use her wedding ring and a small length of thread. You can also buy dowsing pendulums at any new age store.

Once you have your pendulum, hold the end of the cord with the thumb and first finger of your dominant hand. Rest your elbow on a table and allow the pendulum to swing an inch or so above the surface. Deliberately swing the pendulum backward and forward in front of you, and then swing it from side to side. Finally, swing it in circles, both clockwise and counterclockwise. This allows you to get a feel for the four different ways in which the pendulum will respond.

Stop the pendulum's movement with your free hand, and then ask out loud: "Which movement indicates 'yes'?" If you have not experimented with a pendulum before, it might take a minute or two to start moving. Once you gain experience, the movement will be instant. Once you have determined the positive response, ask: "Which movement indicates 'no'?" Follow this with two more questions: "Which movement indicates 'I don't know'?" and "Which movement means 'I don't want to answer'?"

Once you know what each movement means, you can proceed to ask your pendulum questions about anything that can be answered by one of these four responses. You might ask your pendulum if you are male, for instance. If you are, you will receive a "yes" response. Naturally, you will receive a "no" response if you are not. It is a good idea to test yourself with questions that you already know the answers to, as this helps to build up your confidence in the answers provided by the pendulum.

When you feel ready, you can start asking questions about anything at all. If you are using the pendulum to help balance your chakras, you can start asking: "Is my root chakra in balance?" Make a note of the answers as you ask about each chakra in turn. Let's assume that you receive a positive response to all the chakras, except one. Let's assume that the solar plexus chakra is out of balance. Now that you know this, you can do something about it. Ask the pendulum if this chakra is understimulated. Obviously, if the answer is "no," the chakra is overstimulated. However, it is a good idea to ask your pendulum to confirm that for you.

You know that the color for this chakra is yellow. If this chakra is understimulated, you need more yellow in your system. You can achieve this by wearing something that is yellow, carrying a yellow crystal, such as citrine or calcite, or eating and drinking yellow foods. You can also look at a wall or painting that is largely yellow. A good method is to close your eyes and visualize yourself taking in deep breaths of yellow. Imagine the yellow energy spreading throughout your body, and especially to the area of your solar plexus chakra. Hold each breath for several seconds, and then exhale slowly. When you feel you have absorbed enough yellow energy, which is usually after several deep breaths, test your chakras again. Keep doing this until the pendulum gives a positive reading.

If this chakra is overstimulated, you need do a similar exercise, but this time breathe in the color of the chakra immediately above the chakra you are balancing. In this instance, you will breathe in green energy.

Chakra Cleansing

This highly beneficial exercise will provide you with a sense of well-being, vitality, radiant health, and contentment.

Sit or lie down quietly, and take several slow deep breaths. When you feel ready, take a slow, deep breath and visualize it going to the area of your root chakra. Feel it cleansing and filling the chakra. Hold the breath for several seconds and exhale slowly. Repeat with all of the other chakras.

Once you have done this, you can move on to the next

stage. Visualize yourself breathing in pure red energy, and send this down to your root chakra. Again, hold the breath and exhale slowly. Take a second deep breath of red, and send this to your root chakra. Exhale slowly.

Now take in two breaths of orange energy and send this to your sacral chakra. Repeat with each of the other chakras. By the time you have done this, you will have absorbed into your chakras all the colors of the rainbow.

Gabriel and the Sacral Chakra

Gabriel is involved with the sacral chakra because of her interest in purification. If you have been sexually abused, or are constantly filled with negative sexual thoughts, Gabriel can help you by harmonizing this chakra. Likewise, if your body is full of toxins, Gabriel can use this chakra to help eliminate them. Because the sacral chakra is related to the water element, these toxins can be in any part of your body. If you have taken on too many problems that are not rightfully yours, Gabriel can use this chakra to help you eliminate them. If you have a negative attitude or approach to every aspect of your life, Gabriel can stimulate this chakra to enable you to enjoy life again.

You need to create a ritual for yourself if you want to eliminate these difficulties. What you do is entirely up to you, but the most important aspect of it is that you surround yourself with orange energy and then have a conversation with Gabriel. You might like to start with an orange bubble bath to physically purify yourself. If you cannot do that, perhaps you could find some orange-colored soap to wash yourself with. You might find an orange-colored gown or robe to wear while performing this ritual. (I have a friend who has seven robes, one of each color of the rainbow. Whenever he feels the need of a certain color, he wears that particular robe until he feels balanced again.)

You will probably want to use at least one orange candle. Gather together a few items that are orange in color, and attractive to you. You can use orange-colored fruit and vegetables, if you wish. You might prefer orange-colored hand-kerchiefs or scarves. You might have some small orange-colored ornaments that could be used.

Arrange these items in a circle. This circle needs to be large enough for you to sit or lie down inside it. Wear your orange robe, if you have one. If not, wear comfortable, loose-fitting clothes, or work skyclad.

Light the candles, if you are using them. As you will have your eyes closed for most of this ritual, make sure that they are in secure candle holders.

Make yourself comfortable in the center of the circle. Close your eyes and think of the color orange. See what associations come into your mind. You might feel friendliness, creativity, confidence, and other positive words. However, because of what you have been through, it is just as likely that you will think negative thoughts about this color. You might feel sorry for yourself, and be full of thoughts of self-loathing and disgust. These feelings are fine, as this ritual is intended to help you get rid of them.

When new ideas cease coming to you, focus on relaxing

your body as much as possible. Once you are totally relaxed, ask Gabriel to join you. Welcome her when you feel her presence. Speak out loud, if possible. Explain why you are in an orange circle, and tell her what you desire. (The keywords for the sacral chakra are "I desire.") It is perfectly all right to express your emotions while talking with Gabriel. Tell her everything that happened to make you feel the way you do. It might be difficult to put all of it into words, but Gabriel will understand what you are saying.

The next stage can be difficult. You need to forgive everyone who was involved in whatever happened to you. You cannot get on with your life until you let go of the past. That is why this step is so important. If you find it impossible to do this, thank Gabriel for her help, and tell her that you will do this ritual again later. It makes no difference if you do this ritual once, or twenty times. What matters is that you ultimately free yourself of the heavy load you have been carrying. An extra day, week, or month is not going to make much difference in the grand scheme of things.

If you were able to genuinely and sincerely forgive everyone, you can continue with the ritual.

Take a slow deep breath, while focusing on your root chakra. Visualize yourself being filled with grounding, regenerating, revitalizing red energy. On the second deep breath, focus on your sacral chakra, and imagine yourself being filled with a purifying, supportive orange energy. Focus on your solar plexus chakra while taking a third deep breath. This time picture yourself being filled with the life-giving color of the sun. On the fourth deep breath focus on your heart chakra, and feel yourself being filled with a loving, healing energy that is like balm to your entire body. On the fifth deep breath, focus on your throat chakra as you fill yourself with blue energy that enables you to speak openly and freely at any time. On the next breath focus on your third eye chakra as you fill yourself with clairvoyant indigo energy. Finally, focus on your crown chakra as you breathe in pure violet energy. Feel yourself loving everything in the universe, and being loved equally in return.

Finally, ask Gabriel for divine forgiveness, for you and everyone on the planet. Rest quietly for several minutes, realizing that you live in the light, and that your spiritual and physical selves are both part of the eternal. Your physical body will eventually die, but your spiritual self is immortal. With Gabriel's help, you can accomplish anything.

Before getting up, visualize the circle of orange items around you. Allow yourself to feel their energy and enjoy the knowledge that you are now purified and restored in mind, body, and soul. Mentally allow a circle of white light to come down and infuse every cell of your body. This helps to balance your body, just in case you may have absorbed too much of any one color. Thank Gabriel for her help. Take three slow, deep breaths and then open your eyes.

You may feel slightly lightheaded after this exercise. If this is the case, touch the ground, hug a tree, or hold your crystal for a few minutes until you feel calm and relaxed. When you feel ready, carry on with your day.

The Brow Chakra

Gabriel is also responsible for the brow chakra. This is known as the third eye or Christ-consciousness chakra. In the East it is called *ajna*, which is the Sanskrit word for "to perceive." Your brow chakra is your psychic center. Gabriel will help you open your third eye to achieve greater vision and insight. She will help you develop your skills of telepathy, clairvoyance, and precognition. She can also give you regular guidance through this chakra.

You will need to either stand or sit in a straight-backed chair for this exercise. Some people prefer to rest their spines against the back of the chair, while others prefer to sit on the edge of the chair. The important thing is for your spine to be straight while doing this exercise.

Close your eyes and take three slow breaths. Each exhalation should sound like a sigh. Mentally surround yourself in pure, white light, and enjoy the feeling of warmth, security, and protection it gives you. Visualize a small orb of violet energy coming down from the heavens and into your body through the top of your head. Sense it coming to rest in the center of your head, in the area of your brow chakra. Feel it enriching and empowering your brow chakra as it fills with pure violet light and energy.

When you feel ready, ask Gabriel to join you. Thank her for all the blessings she has provided you with, and ask her to help you develop your intuitive awarenesses. You will feel her response in your brow chakra.

Once you have received a positive response, rub your hands briskly together for thirty seconds and then cup them over each eye. Your eyes are still closed at this stage. After thirty seconds, open your eyes and slowly remove your hands. You may see the white light you have surrounded yourself with. You may even see Gabriel. What you are most likely to feel is a sensation in your third eye. It will be an awareness that you can now see well beyond the mere physical world, and have access to additional insights and perceptions whenever you wish.

Close your eyes again, and focus your attention on your brow chakra. Think about something you will be doing in the next week or so. Ideally, this should be a pleasurable activity. Go through the entire experience in your mind's eye, with everything occurring in exactly the way you would like it to be.

Once you have gone through this scenario, let it go, and bring your attention back to the present. Visualize a stream of white light entering the top of your head and going down through each chakra in turn, washing and purifying them. Thank Gabriel for the gifts of vision, clarity, clairvoyance, and precognition. Thank her for being willing to help you interpret your visions, dreams, and psychic perceptions. Finally, thank her for her continued support.

When you feel ready, open your eyes. Take a few minutes to become familiar with your everyday world, and then carry on with your day.

You can repeat this exercise as frequently as you wish. Pay special attention to the future event that you visualized, and see if everything occurred exactly as in the meditation. Your accuracy rate will increase each time you perform this exercise.

In the next chapter we will look at Gabriel's role in the Kabbalah. The Tree of Life in the Kabbalah is a symbol that connects God, mankind, angels, and other beings. All four archangels play an important role in this.

Ten

GABRIEL AND THE TREE OF LIFE

THE *Kabbalah* is an esoteric system of Jewish mysticism that was devised to gain knowledge of God. The word Kabbalah comes from the Hebrew, and means "that which is received." No one knows where it came from originally, although tradition provides two intriguing accounts of how it may have originated. The version I prefer is that the Kabbalah was given to Adam in the Garden of Eden by the Archangel Gabriel. The second version says that it was given to Moses by the Archangel Metatron. The original information came from the angelic kingdom in both accounts, but unfortunately, neither story is correct. The Kabbalah is derived from an oral tradition called *Merkava*, dating back to the first century CE, that involved contemplation of the divine throne or chariot (Merkava) seen by the prophet Ezekiel in his vision (Ezekiel 1: 1–28).

At some stage between the third and sixth centuries, a book called *Sefer Yetzira*, or *Book of Formation*, appeared. This book taught that creation occurred when ten emanations called sephiroth mixed with the twenty-two letters of the Hebrew alphabet. These were called the *thirty-two paths of secret wisdom*, and together form what is known as the Tree of Life. Amazingly, this simple diagram of the Tree of Life manages to symbolize the entire universe.

The Tree of Life is comprised of ten sephiroth, or spheres, with twenty-two paths or lines connecting them. The word "sephiroth" (or "sephirah," singular) comes from a Hebrew word meaning sapphire, and this word was presumably chosen to demonstrate the glory and radiance of God. The ten spheres represent states of being, while the twenty-two paths symbolize states of becoming. The symbology of the Tree of Life gradually evolved and developed over the centuries, and first appeared in its final form in 1652.

The tree contains three pillars. On the left side is the Pillar of Severity, which is passive and negative in nature. On the right is the Pillar of Mercy, which is both positive and active. The middle pillar is the Middle Way, or equilibrium. This represents a path through life that recognizes the two extremes, but refuses to give in to them.

Each sephirah has a particular set of associations:

1. *Kether*, the Crown. Archangel: Metatron, Angel of the presence. Highest angelic world: God. Planet: Uranus. Zodiac: Aquarius. Gemstone: Diamond.

2. *Chokmah*, Wisdom. Archangel: Raziel, Herald of God. Highest angelic world: Seraphim. Planet: Pluto.

Zodiac: Scorpio. Gemstone: Turquoise. The great father.

3. *Binah*, Understanding. Archangel: Tzaphqiel, Concern of God. Highest angelic world: Cherubim. Planet: Neptune. Zodiac: Pisces. Gemstone: Pearl. The great mother.

4. *Chesed*, Mercy. Archangel: Tzadqiel, Justice of God. Highest angelic world: Thrones. Planet: Jupiter. Zodiac: Sagittarius. Gemstone: Sapphire.

5. *Geburah*, Strength. Archangel: Kamael, Severity of God. Highest angelic world: Dominions. Planet: Mars. Zodiac: Aries. Gemstone: Ruby.

6. *Tiphareth*, Beauty. Archangel: Michael, Like unto God (interchangeable with Raphael, Healer of God). Highest angelic world: Virtues. Planet: Sun. Zodiac: Leo. Gemstone: Topaz.

7. *Netzach*, Victory. Archangel: Haniel, Pleasure of God (interchangeable with Uriel, Light of God). Highest angelic world: Powers. Planet: Venus. Zodiac: Taurus and Libra. Gemstone: Emerald.

8. *Hod*, Splendor. Archangel: Michael, Like unto God (interchangeable with Raphael, Healer of God). Highest angelic world: Principalities. Planet: Mercury. Zodiac: Gemini and Virgo. Gemstone: Opal.

9. *Yesod*, Foundation. Archangel: Gabriel, Strength of God. Highest angelic world: Archangels. Planet: Moon. Zodiac: Cancer. Gemstone: Quartz.

10. *Malkuth*, Kingdom. Archangel: Sandalphon, World
    Prince on Earth. Highest angelic world: Angels.
    Planet: Saturn. Zodiac: Capricorn. Gemstone: Rock
    crystal.

To complicate matters still further, each sephirah exists
simultaneously in four different worlds. There is the world
of Assiah, or the material, physical world that we are all living in. Assiah's element is, not surprisingly, earth. Yetzirah,
the formative world, is one step higher and is the realm of
angels. Yetzirah's element is air. Briah is the creative, receptive world and is the home of the archangels. Briah's element is water. Finally, Atziluth, the archetypal world, is the
abode of God. Its element is fire.

The fact that these four worlds exist in each sephirah is
important. It means that angels, archangels and God can be
found in Malkuth, at the bottom of the Tree of Life, exactly
as they are in Kether, the highest sephirah.

The Hermetic Order of the Golden Dawn came up with
their own set of color correspondences for each of the four
worlds:

Atziloth

1. Kether, the Crown: Brilliance

2. Chockmah, Wisdom: Sky blue

3. Binah, Understanding: Crimson

4. Chesed, Mercy: Deep violet

5. Geburah, Strength: Orange

6. Tiphareth, Beauty: Clear pink rose

7. Netzach, Victory: Amber

8. Hod, Splendor: Violet

9. Yesod, Foundation: Indigo

10. Malkuth, Kingdom: Yellow

Briah

1. Kether, the Crown: White brilliance

2. Chockmah, Wisdom: Gray

3. Binah, Understanding: Black

4. Chesed, Mercy: Blue

5. Geburah, Strength: Scarlet

6. Tiphareth, Beauty: Yellow

7. Netzach, Victory: Emerald

8. Hod, Splendor: Orange

9. Yesod, Foundation: Violet

10. Malkuth, Kingdom: Citrine

Yetzirah

1. Kether, the Crown: White brilliance

2. Chockmah, Wisdom: Mother-of-pearl gray

3. Binah, Understanding: Brown

4. Chesed, Mercy: Deep purple

5. Geburah, Strength: Bright scarlet

6. Tiphareth, Beauty: Salmon

7. Netzach, Victory: Yellow-green

8. Hod, Splendor: Red russet

9. Yesod, Foundation: Deep purple

10. Malkuth, Kingdom: Citrine, black-flecked gold

Assiah

1. Kether, the Crown: White-flecked gold
2. Chockmah, Wisdom: White-flecked red
3. Binah, Understanding: Gray-flecked pink
4. Chesed, Mercy: Deep azure-flecked yellow
5. Geburah, Strength: Red-flecked black
6. Tiphareth, Beauty: Gold amber
7. Netzach, Victory: Olive-flecked gold
8. Hod, Splendor: Yellow-brown-flecked white
9. Yesod, Foundation: Citrine-flecked azure
10. Malkuth, Kingdom: Black-rayed yellow

The Flashing Tablets

In Kabbalistic philosophy everything comes originally from an unmanifested state that is beyond human comprehension. From this negative emptiness came the ten positive sephiroth, or ten states of being. Each sephirah is connected with all the others, but also is unique and complete in itself.

The moment of creation can be visualized with divine energy coming down through the Tree of Life from Kether to Malkuth in a zig-zag pattern, known as the Flaming Sword, or Lightning Flash.

From this original Lightning Flash came the Flashing Tablets, which are used for meditation purposes. They work by using complementary colors that create an optical illusion that seems to "flash" in front of the eyes.

These tablets are usually constructed to help people gain access to the energies of the sephiroth. However, by making a tablet that represents the energies of Yesod, which is ruled by Gabriel, we can also gain instant access to her, and her divine energy.

To do this, you need a sheet of cardboard, about 8½ by 11 inches. On this draw a design that is pleasing to you. In a sense, this is a type of mandala, and you might choose to start with a circle and then create a design inside it. You might like to have a nine-sided shape in the center of a square. This is because Yesod is the ninth sephirah. However, whatever you choose to do is up to you. Make sure the design is reasonably simple, as the next stage is to color it in. Once you have drawn the design, use a violet-colored felt tip marker to fill in approximately half of the design. Violet is used because it is the color of Briah (the home of the archangels) in Yesod. Use a citrine or pale-yellow-colored marker to fill in the other sections. Citrine is the color of Assiah, or the material world, in Yesod. If you prefer, you can use a flashing tablet from a book such as *Western Mandalas of Transformation* by Soror A. L.[1]

Once the tablet has been made, it needs to be charged and consecrated. This is to purify and dedicate the tablet for its purpose. The best time to consecrate any magical implement designed to help your relationship with Gabriel is on the full moon. If possible, perform the consecration outdoors, under the full moon. Alternatively, you can perform it indoors, near a window that allows you to see the moon.

All four elements are used in the consecration. You will need some salt, or fresh earth, to symbolize the earth element, a glass of water for the water element, stick incense for air, and a violet or white candle for fire (use as many candles as you wish).

Arrange these implements in front of you and light the candle and the incense. Hold the tablet up to the moon, allowing it to be exposed to the moonlight. Set the tablet down in front of you, and ask Gabriel to bless it for you. Wait until you feel a response. Then say out loud: "I bless you with energy from the earth." Sprinkle a small amount of salt, or earth, over the tablet. "I bless you with the energy of water." Dip a finger into the glass of water and allow a drop or two to fall onto the tablet. "I bless you with the energy of fire." Pick up the tablet and pass it around the candle flame in a clockwise circle. "I bless you with the energy of air." Pass the tablet through the smoke coming from the incense.

Hold the tablet up to the light of the moon again, and say: "Thank you (God, universal energy, or whoever else you wish to thank), for allowing me to consecrate and purify this flaming tablet. I dedicate this tablet to Archangel Gabriel. It will be used only for good, and will help me to maintain a constant, close relationship with Gabriel." Place the tablet down, and gaze up at the moon. "Thank you, Gabriel, for always being there for me."

The tablet has now been consecrated and is ready for use. The ritual is over, and the implements need to be put away carefully. When doing something of this sort, I sometimes keep the incense and candle burning for a while afterward.

Place the tablet at eye-level and sit down comfortably a few feet away from it. Close your eyes and visualize yourself surrounded by a protective white light. Gaze directly at the center of the sheet of cardboard. You will naturally focus on the violet color. Do not shift your gaze to look at other parts of the design. Remain focused on the center, even if your eyes become tired. After a minute or two, your eye muscles will relax and the citrine will take over as the dominant color. As this happens, the two colors will start to flicker from one to the other, and you will understand why these are called "flashing" tablets.

If the flashing effect does not occur after a few minutes, close your eyes. You should see in your mind's eye an after image of the citrine (the opposite color to the one you were focusing on). If this does not occur, open your eyes and gaze at the picture again for thirty seconds, and then see what happens. If you still have no success, experiment by sitting a little bit closer, and if necessary, further away, from the picture.

Once you receive the flashing effect, you will find it hard to remain focused. Continue staring at the picture, with your mind in a relaxed, contemplative state. After a few minutes, your eyes will feel tired and will close of their own accord. You will still see the tablet in your mind. Visualize it coming closer and closer to you until it finally absorbs you, and you are totally surrounded by it.

You are now inside Yesod, and you can start talking to Gabriel. Your clairvoyant sense, coupled with the magic of the flashing tablet, and the fact that you have entered Yesod, will enable you to enjoy a remarkably close encounter with Gabriel. You may even see her. If you see her, you may find she looks quite different from what you imagined. In Yesod, the element is water and the planetary correspondence is the moon. Both of these are feminine, one of the reasons why I chose to call Gabriel "she" in this book. Inside Yesod, you will be able to enjoy a detailed, insightful conversation with her in a matter of seconds. You will sense her desire to help you find your true calling, and she may give you suggestions in that regard. When the conversation is over, Gabriel will gradually disappear, and you will find the image of the tablet fading in your mind. Familiarize yourself with your surroundings again, and then open your eyes.

Members of the Golden Dawn used these tablets to develop their powers of clairvoyance, and to gain access to the particular sephirah that the tablet represented. Once they had done this, they would invoke the power of the sephirah and ask for strength to accomplish a particular purpose. We have been using just one of the tablets to gain a closer connection with Gabriel. You are likely to find, after using it for a while, that you have picked up valuable insights concerning Yesod, and will want to study further the Kabbalah and the Tree of Life.[2]

Your flashing tablet has been consecrated, and you have a duty to look after it. You might like to keep it permanently on a wall, so that you see it several times a day. If you do this, it will also serve as a silent affirmation of what you are doing, and will help you remain in constant contact with Gabriel. However, as your tablet is consecrated and needs to be respected, you might prefer to put it away carefully when you are not using it.

If at any time you wish to dispose of it, for any reason, you must remove the consecration from the tablet. Place the tablet on your altar or table. Face the east, with one arm stretched out in front of you. Say out loud: "May the mighty archangel Raphael bless me, and protect me from all evil coming from the east."

With your arm still outstretched, turn to face the south. "May the mighty archangel Michael bless me, and protect me from all evil coming from the south."

Turn to the west. "May the mighty archangel Gabriel bless me, and protect me from all evil coming from the west."

Turn to face the north. "May the mighty archangel Uriel bless me, and protect me from all evil coming from the north."

Pick up the tablet and show it to all four directions, starting in the east. When you have done this, replace it on your altar and speak to it. Thank it solemnly for the help it has been to you. Explain why you are removing the consecration. You may have made a new tablet, or perhaps you have found a way of communicating with Gabriel that is better and easier for you. Maybe you simply do not enjoy working with flashing tablets. It makes no difference what the reason is, but you must explain it to the tablet.

Finally, thank the archangels in reverse order, starting with Uriel in the north, followed by Gabriel, Michael and Raphael. The tablet is now deconsecrated, and you can burn it, or dispose of it in any other way that feels right for you.

Eleven

CONCLUSION

GABRIEL has always been one of the more popular archangels. This is because of her feminine, caring, intuitive nature. However, she is just as strong and powerful as the others. Origen called her "the angel of war" in *De Principis,* 1:81. In her career, she has been an angel of vengeance and death, and also the angel of the Annunciation and the Resurrection. In Jewish legend, it was Gabriel who destroyed Sodom and Gomorrah. However, it was this same Gabriel who inspired Joan of Arc to go to the aid of the king of France, and to help the Dauphin.

We usually think of Gabriel as God's messenger. However, of equal importance to this is her role as ambassador to the human race. Because of this, she is willing to help you at any time. However, you must also play your part. You need to work diligently at solving your own problems. Most of the time you will not need Gabriel's help. You should call on her only if you find yourself caught up in a problem that is too difficult for you to handle on your own.

Naturally, you should call on her when you need guidance. Again, however, the matter needs to be important. There is no need to consult Gabriel to determine which movie to see on Saturday night. It is a different matter entirely if you have been offered a position in another city and are not sure whether or not to accept the offer.

Purification is another area where Gabriel can help you enormously. If you need purification for any reason whatsoever, you should not hesitate to ask Gabriel for help.

The major benefits of a close relationship with Gabriel are the insights, visions, inspiration, clairvoyance, and prophecy that she will willingly provide.

Gaining contact with Gabriel will enhance every area of your life. You will feel more confident, more capable, and more aware of every aspect of your life once you get to know her. I hope this book has helped you in this quest, and that experimenting with the ideas and exercises will help you gain a close, loving, and intimate relationship with Gabriel, and the entire angelic kingdom.

May the angels bless you, and surround you with goodness and love, always.

Notes

Introduction

1. Louis Ginzberg, *The Legends of the Jews*, Volume 1, translated by Henrietta Szold (Philadelphia, PA: The Jewish Publication Society of America, 1909), 189.

2. In this book I refer to Gabriel as female. Because of her role as protector of pregnancy and childbirth, Gabriel is usually considered feminine. However, angels are considered sexless (Matthew 22:30), and whenever they appear in human form in the Bible they are always male. Artists frequently depict angels as beautiful women or healthy infants. However, in reality, angels are usually seen as bright, shining beings, rather than as people.

3. Dante Alighieri, *The Divine Comedy*. Originally written in Italian between 1300–1321. Many translations available. *The Divine Comedy* is considered one of the world's greatest poems. It is a vision in which Dante visits Hell, Purgatory, and Heaven.

4. Harold Bloom, *Omens of the Millenium: The Gnosis of Angels, Dreams and Resurrection* (New York, NY: Riverhead Books, 1996), 42.

Chapter One

1. Anonymous, *History of Joseph the Carpenter* in J. L. Warr, *Christian Pseudepigraphic Texts*, edited by Lionel Sumner (Edinburgh, Scotland: Seager and Sons, 1911). In this book, Gabriel is also referred to as "the prince of the angels." However, later in the same book this title is also given to Michael. In Jewish angelology, Michael is considered superior to Gabriel, and would be the only archangel worthy of the title "prince." This also relates to Daniel 12:1: "And at that time shall Michael stand up, the great prince which standeth for the children of thy people."

2. The text of this prayer is: "Hail Mary, full of grace, the Lord is with you. Blessed are you among women and blessed is the fruit of your womb, Jesus. Holy Mary, Mother of God, pray for us sinners, now and at the hour of our death. Amen."

3. Jocelyn Rhys, *The Reliquary: A Collection of Relics* (London, UK: Watts and Company, 1930), 79.

4. Anonymous, *Apophthegmata Patrum*. Translated by B. Ward, and quoted in B. Ward, *The Wisdom of the Desert Fathers* (Oxford, UK: Fairacres Press, 1975), 50.

5. James R. Lewis and Evelyn Dorothy Oliver, *Angels A to Z* (Detroit, MI: Gale Research Inc., 1996), 171.

6. Te Ua Haumene, quoted in *Like Them That Dream: The Maori and the Old Testament* by Bronwyn Elsmore (Tauranga, NZ: The Tauranga Moana Press, 1985), 109.

7. Maulana Muhammad 'Ali, *The Religion of Islam: A Comprehensive Discussion of the Sources, Principles and Practices of Islam* (United Arabic Republic: National Publication and Printing House, n.d.), 178.

8. Al-Baghawĭ, *Masābĭh al-Sunna*, Volume 2 (Cairo, Egypt: Khairiya Editions, 1900), 170.

9. Shaykh Muhammad Hishim Kabbani, *Angels Unveiled: A Sufi Perspective* (Chicago, IL: Kazi Publications, Inc., 1995), 18–19.

10. Louis Ginzberg, *The Legends of the Jews*, Volume 2, translated by Henrietta Szold (Philadelphia, PA: The Jewish Publication Society of America, 1920), 72.

11. Ruzbehan Baqli, quoted in *Angels: Messengers of the Gods* by Peter Lamborn Wilson (London, UK: Thames and Hudson Limited, 1980), 41.

12. Gershom G. Scholem, translated by Ralph Manheim, *On the Kabbalah and its Symbolis*m (New York, NY: Schocken Books, 1965), 147–148. Originally published by Rhein-Verlag, Zurich, 1960.

13. Louis Ginzberg, *The Legends of the Jews*, Volume 2, 362.

14. J. T. Milik (editor), *The Books of Enoch: Aramaic Fragments of Qumrân Cave 4* (Oxford, UK: Oxford University Press, 1976), 231. See also: Matthew Black, *The Book of Enoch or 1 Enoch* (Leiden, Netherlands, 1985), 37.

15. Matthew Bunson, *Angels A to Z* (New York, NY: Crown Trade Paperbacks, 1996), 81 and 115.

16. Louis Ginzberg, *The Legends of the Jews*, Volume 3, translated by Henrietta Szold (Philadelphia, PA: The Jewish Publication Society of America, 1911), 231–232.

17. Louis Ginzberg, T*he Legends of the Jews*, Volume 5, translated by Henrietta Szold (Philadelphia, PA: The Jewish Publication Society of America, 1925), 71.

18. John Dee, quoted in Benjamin Woolley, *The Queen's Conjuror: The Life and Magic of Dr. Dee* (London, UK: HarperCollins, 2001), 238.

19. Christopher Knight and Robert Lomas, *Uriel's Machine* (Gloucester, MA: Fair Winds Press, 2001), 135.

20. Theolyn Cortens, *Living With Angels: Bringing Angels into Your Everyday Life* (London, UK: Judy Piatkus (Publishers) Limited, 2003), 39–40.

Chapter Four

1. Theron Q. Dumont, *The Solar Plexus or Abdominal Brain* (originally published 1918; republished by Health Research, Pomeroy, WA, n.d.)

Chapter Five

1. E. A. Wallis Budge, *Amulets and Superstitions* (Oxford, UK: Oxford University Press, 1930), 62–67.

2. Bob Brier, *Ancient Egyptian Magic* (New York, NY: William Morrow and Company, Inc., 1981), 194. This book also contains (on page 88) a photograph of four carved wooden knots that were used as amulets.

3. Udo Becker, *The Continuum Encyclopedia of Symbols* (New York, NY: The Continuum Publishing Company, 1994), 166–167.

4. Carol Andrews, *Amulets of Ancient Egypt* (London, UK: British Museum Press, 1994), 44. The burial sites where figure-of-eight knots have been found are Khnumet, Sithathor, Sithathoriunet, Mereret, and Senebtisy.

5. Jack Tresidder, *Dictionary of Symbols* (San Francisco, CA: Chronicle Books, 1998), 116.

6. Zolar, *Zolar's Encyclopedia of Omens, Signs and Superstitions* (New York, NY: Prentice Hall Press, 1989), 220.

7. Carole Porter, *Knock on Wood and Other Superstitions* (New York, NY: Bonanza Books, 1983), 112.

Chapter Six

1. Zolar, *Dreams, Lucky Numbers, Omens, Oils and Incense* (New York, NY: Arco Publishing Company, Inc., 1970), 205.

2. Michael Howard, *Incense and Candle Burning* (London, UK: The Aquarian Press, 1991), 98.

3. Keith Foster, *Perfume, Astrology and You* (Greenford, UK: Sagax Publishing, 1997), 16.

4. One book I particularly recommend is *Natural Magic: Potions and Powers from the Magical Garden* by John Michael Greer (St. Paul, MN: Llewellyn Publications, 2000). Other useful books are: *The Complete Book of Incense, Oils and Brews* by Scott Cunningham (St. Paul, MN: Llewellyn Publications, 1989), and *Wylundt's Book of Insence* by Steven R. Smith (York Beach, ME: Samuel Weiser, Inc., 1989).

Chapter Seven

1. Theodore Besterman, *Crystal-Gazing* (New Hyde Park, NY: University Books, Inc., 1965), 4. (Originally published by William Rider and Son Limited, London, 1924.)

2. Abolgassem Firdausi, *The Sháhnáma of Firdausi,* translated by A. G. Warner and E. Warner (London, UK: T. Werner Laurie, 1905), 317.

3. Damascius, *Vita Isidori,* edited by R. Asmus (Leipzig, 1911), 118.

4. John Potter, *Archaeologia Graeca,* edited by J. Boyd (London, UK: Thomas Tegg, 1837), 327–328.

5. Pausanius, *Description of Greece,* VII. xxi. 12. Translated by Sir J. G. Frazer (London, UK: Macmillan and Company, 1898, 8 volumes), 1. 176, 36–361.

6. J. Raine, "Divination in the Fifteenth Century by Aid of a Magical Crystal." Article in *The Archaeological Journal* (London, UK, 1856), xiii, 372–374.

7. E. Gutch and Mabel Peacock, *Examples of Printed Folk-lore Concerning Lincolnshire* (London, UK: Folk-Lore Society, 1908), 9.

8. Sir Rennell Rodd, *The Customs and Lore of Modern Greece* (Chicago, IL: Argonaut, Inc., 1968), 185. (First published in London, UK, 1892.)

9. J. C. Beugnot, *Life and Adventures of Count Beugnot: Minister of State Under Napoleon,* edited by

Charlotte Yonge (London, UK: Hurst and Blackett, 1871, 2 volumes), i. 205. (Republished by Elision Classics, 2001.)

10. F. A. Swettenham, *Malay Sketches* (London, UK: John Lane, The Bodley Head, 1895), 202–203. (Reprinted by Graham Brasch, Singapore, 1984.)

11. Theodore Besterman, *Crystal-Gazing*, 99.

12. Michael Constantius Psellus, quoted in Charles A. Ward, *Oracles of Nostradamus* (London, UK: Leadenhall Press, 1891), 76.

13. Donald Tyson, *Scrying for Beginners* (St. Paul, MN: Llewellyn Publications, 1997), 93–101.

Chapter Eight

1. George Frederick Kunz, *The Curious Lore of Precious Stones* (Philadelphia, PA: J. B. Lippincott Company, 1913), 96. (Republished by Dover Publications, New York, NY, 1971.)

2. John Arnott MacCulloch (editor), *The Mythology of All Races*, Volume 5 (New York, NY: Cooper Square Publishers, Inc., 1964), 327.

3. Bruce G. Knuth, *Gems in Myth, Legend and Lore* (Thornton, CO: Jewelers Press, 1999), 114.

4. Kunz, *The Curious Lore of Precious Stones*, 229.

5. Anselmus De Boodt, *Gemmarum et Lapidum Historia* (Hanoviae (Hanau): Wechel, 1609). Anselmus de Boodt (1550–1632) was physician to Rudolph II of Prague, and is best known today for his watercolors. His book on gemstones was the most advanced work on the subject at the time. It was also extremely popular, being reprinted three times in the year it was published. De Boodt was curator of Rudolph's mineral collection, and also collected specimens in Germany, Silesia, and Bohemia. (www.serendipitybooks.com/jahnfull.pdf, p 14)

6. George Frederick Kunz, T*he Magic of Jewels and Charms* (Philadelphia, PA: J. B. Lippincott Company, 1915), 158.

7. William Jones, *History and Mystery of Precious Stones* (London, UK: Richard Bentley and Son Limited, 1880), 114.

8. Damigeron, *De Virtutibus Lapidum: The Virtues of Stones,* translated by Patricia P. Tahil (Seattle, WA: Ars Obscura, 1989), 24.

9. Cornelia M. Parkinson, *Gem Magic* (New York, NY: Fawcett Columbine, 1988), 244.

10. Thomas H. Hendley, *Indian Jewelry* (New Delhi: Sagar Publications, 1962), 158. (Originally published in London, 1909.)

Chapter Ten

1. Soror A. L., *Western Mandalas of Transformation* (St. Paul, MN: Llewellyn Publications, 1996.) This book contains detailed instructions on how to make flashing tablets, and also includes a color illustration of the Yesod/Moon flashing tablet.

2. There are thousands of books available on the Kabbalah. However, there are two books that I particular recommend if the subject is new to you. They are: *Magic of Qabalah: Visions of the Tree of Life* by Kala Trobe (St. Paul, MN: Llewellyn Publications, 2001), and *The Chicken Qabalah of Rabbi Lamed Ben Clifford* by Lon Milo Duquette (York Beach, ME: Weiser Books, 2001).

Suggested Reading

'Ali, Maulana Muhammad, *The Religion of Islam: A Comprehensive Discussion of the Sources, Principles and Practices of Islam*. United Arab Republic: National Publication and Printing House, n.d.

Brinner, William M. and Ricks, Stephen D. (editors), *Studies in Islamic and Judaic Traditions*. Atlanta, GA: Scholars Press, 1986.

Cortens, Theolyn. *Living with Angels: Bringing Angels into Your Everyday Life*. London, UK: Judy Piatkus (Publishers) Limited, 2003.

Cunningham, Scott. *The Complete Book of Incense, Oils and Brews*. St. Paul, MN: Llewellyn Publications, 1989.

Davidson, Gustav. *A Dictionary of Angels: Including the Fallen Angels*. New York, NY: The Free Press, 1967.

Dickason, C. Fred. *Angels Elect and Evil.* Chicago, IL: Moody Press, 1975. Revised edition 1995.

Garrett, Duane A. *Angels and the New Spirituality.* Nashville, TN: Broadman and Holman Publishers, 1995.

Ginzberg, Louis, (translated by Szold, Henrietta) *Legends of the Jews* (7 volumes). Philadelphia, PA: The Jewish Publication Society of America, 1925–1938.

Graham, Billy. *Angels.* Dallas, TX: Word Publishing, 1975.

Judith, Anodea. *Wheels of Life: A User's Guide to the Chakra System.* St. Paul, MN: Llewellyn Publications, 1987.

Kabbani, Shaykh Muhammad Hisham. *Angels Unveiled: A Sufi Perspective.* Chicago, IL: Kazi Publications, Inc., 1995.

MacGregor, Geddes. *Angels: Ministers of Grace.* New York, NY: Paragon House Publishers, 1988.

McLean, Adam (editor). *A Treatise on Angel Magic: Being a Complete Transcription of Ms. Harley 6482 in the British Library.* Grand Rapids, MI: Phanes Press, 1990.

Maguire, Henry (editor), *Byzantine Magic.* Washington, D.C.: Dumbarton Oaks Research Library and Collection, 1995.

Scholem, Gershom G. (translated by Manheim, Ralph), *On the Kabbalah and its Symbolism.* New York, NY: Schocken Books, 1965.

Sitchin, Zecharia. *Divine Encounters: A Guide to Visions, Angels and Other Emissaries.* New York, NY: Avon Books, 1996.

Soror A. L. *Western Mandalas of Transformation.* St. Paul, MN: Llewellyn Publications, 1996.

Tyson, Donald. *Scrying for Beginners.* St. Paul, MN: Llewellyn Publications, 1997.

Webster, Richard. *Spirit Guides and Angel Guardians.* St. Paul, MN: Llewellyn Publications, 1998.

Webster, Richard. *Pendulum Magic for Beginners.* St. Paul, MN: Llewellyn Publications, 2002.

Index

ARCHANGEL POSTER OFFER

Grace your wall with an inspiring and beautiful archangel poster

Considered the holy messenger of God,
Gabriel is the Islamic angel of truth, the archangel of
emotions and dreams, and the angel of hope and childbirth.

Posters are 16 x 20 inches,
on high-quality paper with a glossy finish
Also available: Michael • 0-7387-0711-2

ISBN 0-7387-0709-0 • $9.95 each

Visit our website at www.llewellyn.com
Or order by phone, toll-free within the U.S.
1-877-NEW-WRLD (1-877-639-9753)
Price subject to change without notice

Spirit Guides &
Angel Guardians
Contact Your Invisible Helpers

Richard Webster

They come to our aid when we least expect it, and they disappear as soon as their work is done. Invisible helpers are available to all of us; in fact, we all regularly receive messages from our guardian angels and spirit guides but usually fail to recognize them. This book will help you to realize when this occurs. And when you carry out the exercises provided, you will be able to communicate freely with both your guardian angels and spirit guides.

You will see your spiritual and personal growth take a huge leap forward as soon as you welcome your angels and guides into your life. This book contains numerous case studies that show how angels have touched the lives of others, just like yourself. Experience more fun, happiness, and fulfillment than ever before. Other people will also notice the difference as you become calmer, more relaxed, and more loving than ever before.

1-56718-795-1, 368 pp., 5 ³⁄₁₆ x 8   **$12.95**

Michael
Communicating with the Archangel for Guidance & Protection

Richard Webster

Michael is considered the greatest angel in the Christian, Judaic, and Islamic traditions. Throughout the ages, he has appeared as a protector, a messenger, a guide, a warrior, and a healer. In *Michael*, Richard Webster presents a thorough history of this famous archangel and offers simple techniques for contacting him.

Readers are treated to a detailed introduction to Michael and his many appearances. The rest of this practical guide provides a variety of methods for connecting with Michael, petitioning his help, and creating a lasting bond. Through easy-to-perform rituals and meditations—some involving candle magic, crystals, and dreamwork—readers will learn how to get in touch with the Prince of Light for courage, protection, strength, and spiritual guidance.

0-7387-0540-3, 240 pp., 5 ³⁄₁₆ x 8   **$11.95**

Miracles
Inviting the Extraordinary
Into Your Life

Richard Webster

A practical guide to creating miracles. Miracles are possible for everyone. Once you understand the nature of the miraculous and start believing in miracles, you can start producing your very own miracles. You can transform your life with the simple steps in this practical how-to guide.

Bestselling author Richard Webster gives you the tools and techniques you need to become a miracle worker. Learn how to perform a powerful, nearly forgotten Hawaiian ritual to achieve your heart's desire, and how to use automatic writing to receive guidance from your higher self. Also covered in this one-of-a-kind handbook are instructions for creating miracles through white magic, creative intuition, chakra energy, and spell casting.

0-7387-0606-X, 288 pp., 5³⁄₁₆ x 8   **$10.95**

Angels
Companions in Magick

Silver RavenWolf

Angels do exist. These powerful forces of the Universe flow through human history, riding the currents of our pain and glory. You can call on these beings of the divine for increased knowledge, love, patience, health, wisdom, happiness, and spiritual fulfillment. Always close to those in need, they bring peace and prosperity into our lives.

Here, in this complete text, you will find practical information on how to invite these angelic beings into your life. Build an angelic altar, meet the archangels in meditation, contact your guardian angel, create angel sigils and talismans, work magick with the Angelic Rosary, and talk to the deceased. You will learn to work with angels to gain personal insights and assist in the healing of the planet as well as yourself.

Angels do not belong to any particular religious structure—they are universal. They open their arms to humans of all faiths, bringing love and power into people's lives.

1-56718-724-2, 288 pp., 7 x 10, illus.   **$17.95**

Metatron
Invoking the Angel of
God's Presence

Rose Vanden Eynden

With Metatron in your corner, you're only a petition away from a better life. Rose Vanden Eynden may be the first to devote an entire book to this powerful celestial being—revealing his unique place in the angelic realm and demonstrating how to connect with this wise and compassionate archangel.

Metatron's close proximity to the Creator and connection to humanity make him the ideal angelic ally. Representing balance and unity, this angelic force can help in all areas of personal development. You'll also discover how to contact the "Angel of the Presence" through meditation, dreamwork, ritual, and inspirational writing. There are specific ceremonies for building a closer relationship with the Creator, healing on a global scale, balancing masculine and feminine energies, material/spiritual pursuits, and karmic issues.

Also featured is an insightful "Q and A" with Metatron, channeled by the author to answer compelling questions on life, death, faith, and spirit.

0-7387-1343-0, 264 pp., 5 ³⁄₁₆ x 8, bibliog.   **$13.95**

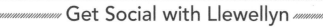

To Write to the Author

Llewellyn Worldwide cannot guarantee that every letter written to the author can be answered, but all will be forwarded. Please write to:

Richard Webster
℅ Llewellyn Worldwide
2143 Wooddale Drive
Woodbury, MN 55125-2989

Please enclose a self-addressed stamped envelope for reply, or $1.00 to cover costs. If outside U.S.A., enclose international postal reply coupon.

Many of Llewellyn's authors have websites with additional information and resources. For more information, please visit our website at http://www.llewellyn.com.